KT-590-937

Contents

Acknowledgements iv

1 Introduction 1

2 Research methods and timetable. 3

3 What is creativity? 5

4 The uses and value of creativity. 9

5 Case study summaries 15

6 What prompts creativity in public services?. 21

7 Creativity in public services: the essential ingredients 25

8 The creative process 31

9 The creative climate: the role of leadership 35

10 Conclusions 39

Appendix A: Case studies. 41

    Aviation Enthusiasts' ID Card 41

    The Camden Boulevard Project 43

    Healthy Eating in Schools. 47

    Manchester City Centre Safe 50

    NHS New Ways of Working. 55

    NHS Direct 60

    Police community support officers 64

    Project 218 67

    St George's Mental Health Trust 70

    The Urban Village 73

Appendix B: Assessing your organisation's potential for creativity 79

Appendix C: Members of the Public Interest Research Group 2003 81

Bibliography. 83

Endnotes. 85

Acknowledgements

This project was initiated by OPM's Public Interest Research Group, a group of people from across public services who advised us that creativity is an issue of increasing importance to the effectiveness of public services, and helped to formulate this research programme on generating creativity for public value. Members of the Public Interest Research Group are listed in Appendix C.

The research would not have been useful without the help of the many people in public service organisations who agreed to be interviewed and the generosity of the many others involved in the case studies. We are grateful to all of them for their time and for sharing their ideas and experiences with us. We would like to say an additional thank you to the small group who came together to discuss the emerging findings. We should add that the interpretations of the case studies' experiences are entirely our own.

Many OPM colleagues contributed to the thinking throughout this project. In particular we thank Diane Beddoes and Gina Cutner who made major contributions to carrying out the case studies, and our Editorial team who produced this report and the website materials.

1 Introduction

Public services cannot stand still for long. When everything around them is changing, they cannot continue to do the same things in the same ways without first considering whether these are the right things to be doing or the right ways in which to be doing them.

Changes in society, and in social expectations and political objectives, produce new needs and problems which public services must address. Even without considering these changes, public services can rarely be confident that they have necessarily found the best approach to dealing with familiar issues. New learning and new technologies, however, offer opportunities to develop different, more effective ways for public services to meet their objectives.

For all these reasons, public services have to be constantly alert to the importance of developing new ways of working. Innovation – both in what is done and how it is done – is a hallmark of any organisation's quest for improved outcomes.

Public services are accountable to the public for the use of public money and for achieving the social results that the public and its representatives demand. In other words, they must search for ways of meeting public and political demands more effectively, while avoiding or limiting negative consequences. They must pursue better value for public money, while limiting innovations that turn out not to be cost-effective. And they must respond to the demand for improvement, while maintaining the positive aspects of the status quo during the period when change is being introduced.

Innovation depends on creativity: the new and imaginative thinking that leads to the development of new approaches, the implementation of new ideas and the achievement of sustained improvement. For public services, creativity is essential to make better use of public money in the achievement of public purposes. But innovation also has to be approached with a careful regard for the risk that it could pose to the well-being of the public it is intended to serve.

Aware of the dilemmas that this tension generates, OPM's Public Interest Research Group posed the question:

> *How can public services generate creativity to produce sustained public value, within a framework of accountability?*

In order to answer this overall question, our research set out to investigate the following specific questions:

- How are creative ideas generated in public services?
- What encourages creativity in public services, and what are the barriers?
- How are creative ideas taken forward to implement innovations that result in improved and sustained social outcomes?

2 Research methods and timetable

Research began in late 2003, following the OPM Public Interest Research Group's choice of research topic earlier that year. The main stages were:

Desk research and literature review

A literature review covered the following topics:

- definitions of creativity;
- the relationship between creativity and innovation;
- creativity in public services: the role and incidence of creativity in public services; policies for creativity in public services; what features of public services encourage and discourage creativity; and
- creativity in other sectors and settings: what encourages and discourages creativity; what purposes does creativity serve?

Development phase interviews

We interviewed members of the Public Interest Research Group, and other people with a particular interest in the field, on the topics covered by the literature review. The 15 interviewees also gave us documented examples of creativity in public services and suggested some undocumented examples as potential case studies.

Research phase interviews

After analysing the development phase interviews, we formulated questions for further exploration in a second round of interviews and in the case studies. The 20 interviewees for this round were working in different public sector settings and roles, including regulation and inspection, senior management, service delivery and front line practice, policy-making, and governance. They were all chosen for their particular interest in or experience of creativity and innovation. They included some people who had played a key part in specific innovations in public services. In these interviews we were able to explore the origins of particular innovations.

Case studies

We scanned the press and other literature to identify potential case studies. We also asked many people working in different contexts in public services, including umbrella and membership bodies, inspectorates, research and policy, and other support organisations, to suggest potential case studies. Our request was based on a simple definition of innovation: something new, different and unexpected that they had seen implemented in a public service setting.

The purpose of the case studies was to develop a detailed understanding of the environmental and other factors that enable or inhibit creativity in public services. Our approach was to identify innovations in public services and to interview the people involved in their origins, development and implementation. In each of the ten case studies we interviewed several people who had each had some involvement in the innovation.

Our emphasis was thus on identifying approaches that seemed to those who suggested them, and to us, to have been new and significantly different at the time they were put into practice. However, it was not possible to rule out the possibility of something very similar having happened elsewhere; indeed, we recognise that creative problem-solving draws on ideas from other contexts in order to develop new approaches, so there would necessarily be connections between the case studies and work elsewhere.

The case studies are summarised on the following pages. They are reported in full in Appendix A. The case studies vary in:

- the type of sector and organisation(s) involved, e.g. the police, local government, NHS hospital trusts
- the scale of the innovation, from national and high profile innovations such as NHS Direct, to local innovations affecting fewer people, such as the school meals service in a primary school
- the purpose and intended outcome, e.g. public safety, children's health
- the activity, e.g. service delivery at the point of interaction with the public, processes inside an organisation or partnership.

Expert seminar

We held an 'expert seminar' in November 2004 to discuss and validate our preliminary conclusions with people who had been involved in the research as interviewees and case studies.

3 What is creativity?

Most people understand creativity, at a general level, to be the process of generating something new or original. Most interpretations view creativity as the bringing together of existing ideas to develop something new and of value. For example, creativity involves: the capacity to think about problems afresh from first principles; to discover common threads amidst the seemingly complex and disparate; to experiment; to dare to be original; to rewrite rules; to visualise future scenarios; and to work at the edge of one's competences rather than at the centre of them.[1]

Robinson[2] describes imagination, the 'capacity to bring into mind conceptions of events, experiences or objects that are not present to the senses', as the foundation of creativity. He also points out that, while imagination is the foundation, creativity is more than this. Creativity means applying imagination to the exploration of problems or possibilities. It is the process of developing original ideas that have value. Thus creativity is a process that:

- is based on imagination or original thinking,
- is purposeful and directed at problem-solving,
- produces ideas that add value.

Creativity and innovation are linked but distinct concepts. 'Creativity can be seen as the development of new ideas, while innovation is the application of those new ideas in practice.'[3] Other sources describe creativity as the readiness and ability to 'see round corners' towards developing novel and innovative solutions.[4][5]

Creativity is not the same as innovation, although creativity is necessary for innovation to take place. Creativity may not result in innovation; creative ideas may or may not be taken forward or implemented in any practical sense. If an idea is implemented, the innovation itself may or may not yield successful outcomes as intended by the creative idea. But creative thinking can also add value by leading to other new thinking, and an unsuccessful innovation can also lead to learning.

How original does creative thinking have to be?

Paul Plsek[6] suggests a 'depth of innovation scale', which is based on the extent to which an idea behind the innovation is unusual or original and makes a large mental leap from what is familiar to a new way of thinking about a problem:

Footnotes can be found at the end of the report (as 'endnotes')

- Usual thinking – the idea is a typical approach, and most people in the same field are already doing something along similar lines
- Potential better practice thinking – the idea is an adaptation of ideas that are emerging in other organisations in the same sector, but is still fairly new.
- Clever thinking – the idea is a clever twist on existing ways of doing things; creative thinking on a small scale.
- Creative connection thinking – the idea is a creative adaptation of ideas that are common outside the sector, but rarely used within it
- Paradigm busting thinking – the idea fundamentally challenges current mental models and paradigms in the sector in an uncommon way.
- Original thinking – the idea is a really new concept; no-one has thought of anything like it before.

The first three points in his scale may give rise to the implementation of change in a particular setting. Only the third of these, 'clever thinking', involves originality and creativity. It is at the fourth point, 'creative connection thinking', that we find the potential to give rise to a radical innovation, which is likely to change fundamentally ways of working or mechanisms for service delivery. Paradigm busting and original thinking can inspire major innovation, which may be systemic, transformative or disruptive. Plsek acknowledges that the rating scale depends to an extent on the knowledge of the people doing the rating, and how much they know about practice across their own and other sectors.

While creativity involves original thinking, it is drawing on things that are already known in order to shape new ideas. Koestler emphasised that creative thinking is a process rather than the apparently random occurrence of a good idea that springs fully formed into someone's mind. 'The creative act is not an act of creation in the sense of the Old Testament. It does not create something out of nothing; it uncovers, selects, reshuffles, combines, synthesises already existing facts, ideas, faculties, skills. The more familiar the parts, the more striking the new whole'.[7]

Creative individuals and creative organisations

As part of its exploration of the role of education in developing creativity, the National Advisory Committee on Creativity, Culture and Education produced a report in which it identified a number of characteristics of creative people. They are curious, they don't always follow rules, they ask unusual questions, they respond to tasks or problems in a surprising way, they challenge conventions and their own and others' assumptions, and they think independently.[8]

The report argued that creativity is not the preserve of the gifted few, but that all young people and adults have creative capacities and that creativity is possible in all areas of human activity. It went on to argue that the education system and approaches to teaching can do a great deal to develop and promote people's creative capacities.

The report suggested that creative people reinterpret and apply their learning in new contexts and communicate their ideas in novel ways. They speculate about and explore possibilities, identify challenges and visualise alternatives, keep their options open, learn to cope with uncertainty and trust their intuition.

Most of the research on creative organisations has taken place in the private sector. This is of limited value to anyone trying to understand what makes a creative public service organisation because, as Hartley notes, 'There are some similarities in innovation processes [between public and private sector organisations] but also distinctive and important differences.'[9] The differences include: the importance of organisational and service innovation, as opposed to product innovation; and the contribution of innovation in public services to public value, as well as to efficiency or to benefits for individuals.

Research in the private sector has highlighted, for example, the importance of people feeling motivated by their work. If people are involved in their work and feel challenged by it, they are more likely to apply creativity, even under pressure.[10] Creativity in a high-pressure environment is possible if the time pressure is interpreted as meaningful urgency, rather than arbitrary deadlines or management pressure.

A clear vision for the organisation is also important. Creativity can be encouraged by ensuring that the organisation's core vision, aims and objectives are clearly defined and effectively communicated. The DTI notes that creativity is enhanced when 'everything is driven by a dynamic vision that everyone has bought into and which captures the imagination of those working in the organisation.'[11]

Some researchers in the private sector have argued in favour of the 'failure-tolerant' leader, 'who, through their words and actions, helps people overcome their fear of failure and, in the process, create a culture of intelligent risk taking that leads to sustained innovation.' Their aim is to encourage employees not to think in terms of success or failure, but in terms of learning and experience.[12]

Our research aims to draw on this previous research, which has focused mainly on the private sector, and to redress the previous balance by exploring how creativity can be developed in public service organisations and put to good use for public purposes.

photo: © Paul Campbell; stock.xchng

photo: © Diego Ortega; stock.xchng

4 The uses and value of creativity

The influence of organisational purpose

Creativity is about applying imagination to the exploration of problems and possibilities and thereby developing ideas that have value. Creativity is often associated only with the arts, rather than with all areas of activity. While it is true that originality is at more of a premium in the artistic and cultural sector than elsewhere, the sector does not have an exclusive claim to be described as creative. The value attached to creativity depends on the extent to which it serves the purposes of an organisation or activity.

In public services, the value of creativity comes, ultimately, from its contribution to the services' intended outcomes, such as improved health and more sustainable communities, improved relationships involving trust and participation in public governance, greater public and user satisfaction and improved value for money for public spending. In other sectors, the value of productivity comes from its contribution to other purposes. In the private sector, for example, creativity is of value when it contributes to the satisfaction of customers but also, fundamentally, to the profitability of a business.

Organisational purposes, and the systems that hold people accountable for achieving them, influence both the uses and value of creativity. They:

- influence perceptions of what constitutes a problem requiring a solution
- influence the priority given to creative problem-solving
- set up different motivations and incentives to be creative
- place different constraints on innovation, which can also influence the motivation to be creative.

Here we consider briefly the influences on the use and value of creativity in the private sector and in the voluntary and not-for-profit sector before exploring in more detail the influences on the use and value of creativity in public services and how these differ from other sectors.

Creativity for private sector purposes

In the private sector, where the survival and success of a company depends on profitability, creativity is directed toward gaining competitive advantage, and thus maintaining or increasing profitability. The more competitive a field, the more important is creativity to generate and meet consumer demands and improve efficiency.

People working in private sector companies are accountable to their directors, who in turn are accountable to the shareholders or owners. Overall, legal accountability in the private sector is for the longevity and financial success of the company. Thus the private sector tends to be motivated by shareholder value, while the public sector is driven by less easily defined concepts of 'public interest' and/or 'policy objectives.'[13] In a business environment, where gaining a competitive edge establishes a clear incentive for creativity and innovation, fostering new ideas is a key to success.

It can be argued that, in addition to having a direct incentive for innovation, businesses have fewer constraints on their scope for creativity than public services do, and more control over the risk of innovation. Businesses are not limited to any particular field of activity so they have a potentially wide scope for developing new ideas and products, and they can stop providing products or services that are not meeting their objectives. There is scope for generating demand and making a market. It is usually possible to test the market for new products and services before making a major investment, without a risk to the well-being of the public or customers.

Despite the apparent incentives for creativity and innovation, research shows that the commitment to capitalise on innovative ideas is not universal in the private sector. An Industrial Society survey in 2000[14] showed that the majority of respondent companies had no strategy for promoting innovation. Only 16 per cent had a strategy in place, and 25 per cent addressed innovation in an *ad hoc* way. The survey found that while about 70 per cent of respondent organisations encouraged and generated new ideas, only about half had mechanisms to resource and exploit them.

Creativity for voluntary sector purposes

The voluntary and not-for-profit sector comprises a large and diverse group of organisations. These use a variety of organisational forms, which determine their accountability. In general, people are held to account for achieving the organisation's stated social purposes and not primarily for making a profit. Of course, sound financial performance, including the ability to generate surplus that can be re-invested in the organisation's purposes, is important.

Parts of the voluntary and not-for-profit sector have long regarded creativity and innovation as important characteristics of their organisations. Unconstrained by the political direction and control imposed on the statutory sector, they are free, as independent bodies, to develop new ways of working. Creativity can be used to develop new and more effective approaches to meeting their charitable objectives and to demonstrate innovative approaches that they hope others will adopt. Indeed, potential funders are frequently attracted by new ideas and innovations.

In practice, however, there are constraints on creativity, which, as in other sectors, stem from the accountabilities of those running the organisation. The financial survival of the organisation, particularly if it is small, is often a pressing concern and may make decision makers risk-averse. Those who support the organisation with financial donations may be conservative and deterred by the prospect of radical innovation. In addition, many voluntary organisations are funded by the statutory sector to provide specific services. The terms of this funding may prescribe what is to be done and thus limit the scope for creativity.

A large part of the work of the voluntary sector is concerned with vulnerable people and services that can have important human consequences. Where a voluntary organisation decides to stop doing something in order to implement an innovation, it may receive an adverse reaction from its supporters and service users. Many proposed innovations will need to be carefully tested before implementation. So there can be disincentives to being creative and innovative, even where this could serve the organisation's purposes.

Creativity for public service purposes

Public service organisations exist to serve the public interest by producing public value, either directly or indirectly, using public money. 'Public value' includes some measurable outcomes, for example improved educational attainment or an overall reduction in crime levels. It also encompasses outcomes that are more difficult to quantify. These include the accessibility of services, social cohesion, social capital, trust in public institutions and participation in public governance.[15]

Among our case studies, the public value of creativity stemmed from: identifiable and tangible innovations in the services that were provided; innovations in the ways in which people and organisations worked; and from more flexible and appropriate responses to the needs of specific individuals or groups. All of these contribute, ultimately, to the social outcomes achieved by the organisations and others.

Changes in social norms, affected by ideology, culture, developments in the economy and advances in technology, have an impact on the way people live and work and may result in changes to the way they define 'public value'. Changes in patterns of work and family and social relationships will also have an impact. Shifts in the demographic profile, and the increasing diversity within society, make definitions of the 'public interest' complex. With diversity comes a range of different needs and preferences. These can have an impact at a very local level of public service provision, as well as on a much wider scale.

Public services must constantly review their objectives and strategies and sometimes even their purposes in the light of these changes. Changes in demographic composition, public preferences, or mechanisms for provision, for example, may require a review of whether particular aspects of service provision should be improved, reduced, changed or abandoned.[16] Demands for improvement in outcomes, quality and efficiency may prompt the need for change to bring services in line with what the public needs and wants. Service providers must keep challenging themselves to work out the best ways of delivering public value and to guard against complacency or service provision on a 'good enough' basis.

Among the case studies for this research we found creativity was being used to explore:

- possible solutions to old and familiar problems, to which no wholly satisfactory solution has been found;
- possible solutions to new problems, which arise from change within or outside an organisation.

Creativity was also used to explore:

- the use of newly available possibilities (e.g. new technologies) for bringing about desirable change, where the desirable change is due to an underlying or newly discovered problem rather than a pressing one.

These types of problems and possibilities fall into the category of what are sometimes called 'wicked problems'. Back in 1973, Rittel and Webber[17] introduced this phrase – which is now in frequent but loose use in public service parlance – which they used to describe problems that are characteristic of those faced by public policy-makers and public managers and which are particularly intractable or difficult to 'solve'. In doing so, they set out some practical and tangible issues faced by public services, showing that it is not only social and other environmental changes that demand creativity of public services, it is also the wicked nature of the problems they face.

A wicked problem has a number of characteristics. A wicked problem defies efforts to delineate its boundaries or to establish its causes. It can be understood in many different ways and it may be inseparable from other problems. The way in which it is understood, and how wide and far back the understanding goes in trying to understand a web of possible and related causes, establishes the space in which ideas about possible solutions can be sought. Faced with wicked problems, it is always possible imagine a different solution that might be better.

The possibility of understanding a problem in different ways and of improving on ways of dealing with it, provide the motivation to search for better solutions. However, in public services, this motivation for creativity has to be managed within a particular approach to accountability. People in charge of running public services are held to account for producing better outcomes and increasing public value while not taking any decisions that result in damage to individuals or to the public interest.

This sets up a dilemma when managing the search for better solutions to wicked problems. Solutions are difficult to evaluate comprehensively as they can generate consequences (desirable and undesirable) over an extended period of time. There is little opportunity for experiment or trial and error, given that the implementation of solutions influences people's lives, perhaps in a very serious way. The value of possible solutions will depend on the particular perspectives of different interested parties and can be hotly contested. Nor is it possible to be sure that all the potential solutions have been identified and considered, before a judgement has to be made on selection and implementation.

So those in charge of public services must search for better solutions while managing the risks associated with making changes. Change can have significant human consequences as well as financial ones. It is rarely possible for a public service organisation to abandon an existing service while it develops a new approach, or to stop trying to meet a particular need because it has identified a way of meeting a different need more effectively. It is hardly surprising, then, that public service organisations are often described as risk-averse. Indeed, there is every reason why the public should demand a high standard of risk management from its public services. The challenge is in balancing this with the creativity that changes in the public interest also rely on.

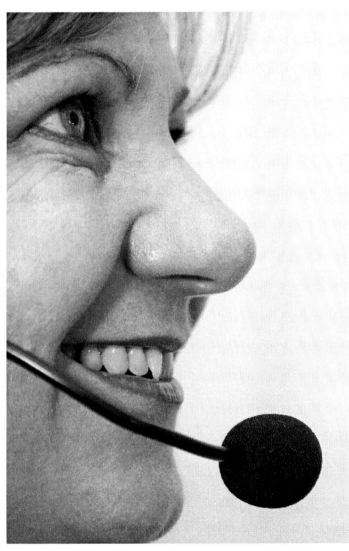

photo: Gloria-Leigh Logan; istockphoto.com

5 Case study summaries

In each of ten case studies we interviewed people involved in the origins of the ideas and in the development and implementation of the innovation. The case studies are summarised here and described more fully in Appendix A. They are:

- **Aviation enthusiasts' ID cards**
- **Camden Boulevard project**
- **Healthy eating in schools**
- **Manchester City Centre Safe**
- **New Ways of Working**
- **NHS Direct**
- **Police community support officers**
- **Project 218, Glasgow**
- **St George's Mental Health Trust**
- **The Urban Village**

Aviation enthusiasts' ID cards

Aviation enthusiasts at Heathrow have become additional 'eyes and ears' of the police during a period of heightened security, instead of being categorised as a security risk and discouraged from pursuing their interest in plane spotting.

In the wake of 11 September 2001, airport security was increased and viewing platforms were closed at several airports, on the advice of the Home Office. Aviation enthusiasts reported a more hostile and suspicious attitude from the police, who frequently moved them away from their usual viewing areas. The chair of the largest

photo: © Paul Campbell; stock.xchng

enthusiasts' organisation wrote to the Commissioner of the Metropolitan Police, noting that there are usually more enthusiasts than police at airports and suggesting that enthusiasts be enlisted as the 'eyes and ears' of the police on the ground. Police, the airport and enthusiasts have since worked together to develop an

ID card for enthusiasts, which gives them access to viewing areas in return for signing up to look out for and report suspicious behaviour. Relations between the police and enthusiasts appear to have improved in some areas as a result.

Camden Boulevard project

The local authority has developed a scheme to improve the environment by encouraging people to blur traditional boundaries between functions, to share responsibilities and to work together to develop new approaches. Within this, an initiative has been developed to deal with many of the small-scale problems that cause public dissatisfaction by inviting community groups to propose, undertake and manage small environmental projects themselves, with local authority funding.

While in-house indicators and inspectorate's reports showed street-scene services to be performing well, public satisfaction was low. The local authority recognised that it could not achieve a 'quantum leap' in public satisfaction with the local street-scene just by making incremental improvements. They gave a manager a specific brief – and budget – to blur boundaries and responsibilities in a quest for new approaches.

One of a number of projects to be developed involves community groups bidding for funding to undertake and manage small projects in their neighbourhoods, such as planting flowers in vacant plots to deter rubbish dumping. The aim was to tackle the small-scale problems that cause dissatisfaction, which the council found it impractical to deal with effectively, and to encourage local people to share responsibility for the local environment.

Healthy eating in schools

Two primary schools in different parts of the country moved from low take-up of nutritionally poor school meals to a self-managed and profitable meals service that provides healthier eating, has improved the children's behaviour, offers educational opportunities and supports the local economy.

photo: © Karen Squires; istockphoto.com

The initiatives in this case study predated the current move to healthier eating in schools, which has government backing in the wake of a 2005 TV series by Jamie Oliver.

The governors and headteachers of these two primary schools recognised that their provision of school meals was of poor quality and uneconomic because of low take-up. They supported catering managers who wanted to stop serving the food provided by the local authority's catering contractor. Food (much of it organic) is now provided by local, independent suppliers; take-up of meals has increased (despite an increase in cost); the children's behaviour has improved; and the meals services generate a small profit, which is reinvested in the kitchens. Local suppliers benefit from the additional business and children visit local farms to learn about food production and healthy eating.

Manchester City Centre Safe

The increase in alcohol-related crime in Manchester prompted the police to take a fresh look at all the causes of the problem and to develop a whole programme of approaches, in partnership with other agencies, that tackle excessive drinking rather than dealing only with the criminal behaviour that results.

This initiative was a response to a crisis – a huge increase in alcohol-related crime in the centre of Manchester in the late '90s, which was fuelling public and political demand for action and was costing the police a great deal of money in overtime pay. Greater Manchester Police recruited two senior people with relevant commercial experience and gave them a remit to develop a fresh approach to the problems, based on a re-examination of the underlying causes. The resulting approach encompasses many different aspects of the night-time economy, including transport and the management of licensed premises, and the participation of many different stakeholders, including the local authority, businesses and bus companies. The police profile within the scheme, which has become a well-known brand, is deliberately kept low.

New Ways of Working

New Ways of Working was one of a number of self-managed teams within the NHS Modernisation Agency. It supported the people delivering services in the NHS to find innovative ways of improving access to, and the quality of, patient services.

a) Frimley Park Hospital NHS Trust

This project set out to improve patient access to care while complying with the Working Time Directive, which limits the number of hours individual members of staff may work and which has a particular impact on the availability of doctors. The project has three strands:

- an additional night nurse practitioner and medical technical assistants (MTAs – 'a cross between nursing and pathology staff') – to support the medical staff 'on-take' team.
- improving patient assessment times and throughput of emergency referrals by installing a series of advanced 'point of care' (PoC) testing equipment
- rearranging doctors' rotas and thereby reducing the number of unsocial hours they work.

b) Newcastle, North Tyneside and Northumberland Mental Health NHS Trust

The fundamental idea behind this project was to re-shape pharmaceutical services and other staff roles in the interests of developing a patient-focused service. The project focused on the roles of the pharmacy staff. The roles of pharmacists and pharmacy technicians were re-defined and the new role of Dispensing Assistant was introduced. Pharmacy services were centred on the ward, rather than being remote from patients, in the dispensary. Pharmacy staff became part of the wider patient care teams.

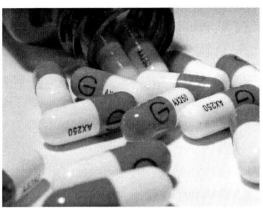

photo: © budgetstockphoto.com

The improved service aimed to provide patients with a seamless pharmacy service, from admission through to discharge.

NHS Direct

NHS Direct was the first service to offer members of the public direct access to health professionals for telephone-based information. It has subsequently expanded into other media.

NHS Direct – the 24-hour telephone help line, staffed by nurses – came into being after the 1997 general election. The new administration asked for proposals for a new idea that would be a high-profile example of the modernisation of the

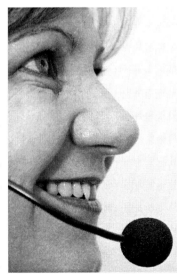

photo: © Gloria-Leigh Logan; istockphoto.com

National Health Service. A small group of people in the Department of Health built on earlier ideas about providing a telephone number for advice when an ambulance was not needed: this idea had been stimulated by the need to reduce pressure on accident and emergency services and out-of-hours GP services. Through a combination of research and public consultation, those involved were able to develop the ideas and to put forward a convincing case to ministers, whose support was essential for the service to be developed. The combination of political and public support, together with evaluation of the pilots, provided the necessary momentum to overcome some reservations among parts of the health professions.

Police community support officers

Police community support officers (PCSOs) work alongside the police, patrolling public spaces and providing reassurance to the public.

photo: detail from Metropolitan Police publicity materials

PCSOs were introduced in London in 2002. The need for heightened security in London after the 11 September attacks in New York stimulated support for ideas that had begun to develop some time before. It had become increasingly evident to some people, most notably the Deputy Commissioner of the Metropolitan Police, that the police could not meet cost-effectively the growing demand for the patrol of public spaces. However, suggestions that this role should be taken on by non-police officers met with considerable suspicion about 'policing on the cheap'. The need for a solution to the security crisis after 11 September provided the opportunity to gain the political support and the resources to develop the detailed proposals that won the acceptance of stakeholders.

Project 218, Glasgow

Women who come into contact with the criminal justice system are offered, as an alternative to custodial sentences, a range of multi-agency services from this newly built facility. The centre aims to help women deal with the problems and situations that lead to re-offending.

A spate of suicides at a Glasgow prison provided the initial impetus for development of a new approach to women offenders. The Time Out centre sets out to tackle the problems of substance misuse and poverty that draw women into and perpetuate offending behaviour. It provides a wide range of services to deal with social, economic and emotional problems, on a residential and non-residential basis, from a building that is well designed, comfortable and attractive. Those involved in the project set out to design a service and facilities that were based on what users wanted and needed, rather than on what was conventionally offered. The project represents the coming together of ministerial policy recommendations and the proven success of a small-scale voluntary sector project. Rolling out the project on a larger scale has required 'selling' its benefits to partner bodies, particularly the criminal justice system, victims of crime and potential service users. Decreasing re-offending rates indicate some success.

St. George's Mental Health Trust

An NHS mental health trust encourages service users to apply for jobs in the organisation and provides support for them in post, with the twin objectives of improving these employees' mental health and addressing shortages of staff.

People with experience of mental health problems are far less likely than others to be employed. Yet research has shown that employment makes an important contribution to good mental health. Following a study visit to the US in the early 1990s, a senior employee at St George's proposed that the trust should reserve current job vacancies for users of mental health services. The scheme at St George's was the first to reserve existing vacancies rather than to create posts specifically for this group of people, as had been done in the US. The aim was to improve the mental health of the employed service users and to help to tackle a shortage of staff in the trust, and more widely in the NHS. Careful piloting and gradual roll out has helped to secure top-level support in the organisation and break down any resistance to the scheme amongst staff, who needed to be convinced that service users could perform effectively in the jobs.

The Urban Village

The Urban Village project addresses the problem of homelessness by recognising that homeless people require support as well as accommodation if they are to improve the quality of their lives and to become independent in the community.

The Urban Village developed from a project in New York, called Common Ground. Crisis, the King's Fund and Genesis Housing, working as a partnership with the support of the Housing Corporation, re-shaped the idea behind Common Ground to fit the specific London context. The Urban Village will provide accommodation for homeless people and low income and key workers within a single building. Training and support will be available to help residents address issues that may affect them as individuals and the community as a whole.

6 What prompts creativity in public services?

Our analysis of the case studies and of our interviewees' experiences shows that, in public services, a range of environmental features or events can prompt creative thinking. These can be internal or external to the setting (the organisation, service or activity) where the creative response develops. They can be dissatisfaction with an existing situation or concern about an emerging one, or the identification and taking of opportunities offered by new developments. Frequently, creativity involves initiating opportunities for change by combining more than one prompt and/or development.

The prompts are, in the internal environment:

- **A crisis or severe problem,**
- **A search for improvement,**
- **A conscious search for a new role or impact,**

and in the external environment:

- **New needs, demands or problems,**
- **New opportunities,**
- **Changes in the wider system of public policy.**

The internal environment

A crisis or severe problem

Where people perceive a problem to be an immediately threat to their ability to continue functioning, or to their other interests, or where performance under existing arrangements is very poor, they may be prompted to look urgently for an alternative.

For the aviation enthusiasts, the tightening of security at the airport presented them with an urgent problem because it threatened to limit the opportunities to pursue their interests. There was a similar urgency for the airport police, as the sudden need to increase security significantly, post 9/11, created additional demands on their resources and existing methods.

Where a problem is greater in breadth or depth from those previously encountered, people may conclude that known approaches do not work and that a new approach to the problem is required. The seriousness of the problem may also mean that they

Unlocking creativity in public services

can more easily justify to others the need for a new approach, and this may also help to prompt or motivate creative thinking.

In Manchester, the increase in alcohol-related crime was so marked, with damaging consequences for public safety and police resources, that the police and partners were prompted to re-think their approach to policing the night-time economy. The Glasgow case study was similar in that ongoing concerns, in this case about the effectiveness of imprisonment for women offenders, were made into a far more pressing problem by a spate of suicides. And in the case of the school meals services, people at the schools had been dissatisfied with the quality of school meals for some time. The threat to the financial viability of the services provided an additional reason for finding a new approach.

A search for improvement

The search for improvement in the outcomes or effectiveness of services was a frequent prompt for creativity. The case studies show that public services can be – and are – creative as part of their core business and mainstream work. The specific prompts for creative thinking include:

- a culture of continuous improvement in an organisation – always trying to find ways of doing things better
- a desire to respond to changing needs and demands
- an improved understanding of public needs and their root causes

The search for improvement was a prompt for creative thinking in the Camden Boulevard project, where there was an ambition to improve on the indifferent or poor levels of public satisfaction with the local environment. Although independent inspections had rated the service highly, the borough wanted to improve further. Similarly, the St George's Mental Health Trust initiative to employ service users was developed from an established and continuing commitment to improving mental health outcomes.

Understanding of the nature of public needs, and their causes, was behind both the development of police community support officers (PCSOs) and the Urban Village project. The PCSO role was invented in response to a growing public demand for greater police presence and visibility on the streets. Understanding the reasons for this demand enabled the Metropolitan Police to develop an alternative to police patrols that met the need expressed by the public. The Urban Village project came from a recognition that homeless people needed more than just accommodation, especially of the type usually provided, if they were to improve the quality of their lives.

A conscious search for a new role or impact

A search for a new role, profile or position in the 'market' or sector can prompt creativity. New partnerships, for example between public and private sector providers, may set out to extend beyond traditional boundaries both what is provided and how it is delivered.[18] New people coming into post, especially into senior positions, may consciously be looking for initiatives that will have an impact on their priority areas.

Among our case studies, NHS Direct provides an example of this. The development was prompted in part by a new government's interest in developing a service within the National Health Service that would strike the public as something new and modern and which would have a direct impact on a large proportion of the population.

The external environment

New needs, demands or problems

Social, economic and political changes result in new needs for and demands on public services. These changes in the external environment are a frequent prompt for creative thinking. The Manchester case study is a good example. A commercially successful night time economy had developed in part of the city, in response to changes in leisure spending and social life. The opening of many new clubs and bars had led to an increase in alcohol-related crime.

New opportunities from an external source

Creative thinking can be prompted by an awareness of new ways of working, especially an awareness of the availability of new technology. The creativity comes in thinking about new ways of employing this technology, often in a new setting. For example, NHS Direct used call centre technology in a way not previously used in the public sector or for health information in the UK.

Changes in the wider system of public policy

Changes in the wider system of public policy, public finance or regulation can produce:

- new opportunities, e.g. to remove barriers to achieving objectives
- new incentives, e.g. reward and recognition for achieving better outcomes
- interventions specifically intended to encourage new approaches to problems
- new difficulties or hurdles.

Any of these can stimulate creativity.

Among the case studies, the New Ways of Working initiative is an example of this prompt. It helped to spur creative thinking at Frimley Park hospital in response to the Working Time Directive, a change in regulation that made it necessary to change working patterns. And at St George's hospital in Morpeth, part of a mental health trust, it set in motion a re-shaping of pharmaceutical services to provide a seamless service to the patient.

The combined effect of more than one prompt for creativity

In most cases there are a number of prompts for creativity, often including both internal and external factors. For example, the search for improvement coincides with a recognition of new or previously unknown problems external to the organisation, or picks up on new opportunities such as the application in other settings of new technologies. Similarly, a crisis can be used to make new opportunities for creativity in collaboration with others. Where a crisis coincides with the recognition of problems in another service area, such as new and changing demands, people may be more motivated to work with others in developing new solutions that will be mutually beneficial.

Thus different combinations of internal and external factors and events can stimulate creativity, but the presence of these prompts is no guarantee of creativity. Creative thinking may or may not develop in response to these factors at any particular time and place. The reasons for the development of a creative response – or otherwise – are explored in the following sections of this report.

photo: © Karen Squires; istockphoto.com

7 Creativity in public services: the essential ingredients

Our analysis of the case studies, which was supported by the analysis of our interviewees' experiences, showed there to be seven elements involved in the application of imagination to the exploration of problems or possibilities. All of these are present where creativity emerges and develops. They form the essential ingredients of creativity in public services:

- **curiosity**
- **motivation**
- **long-term vision of better outcomes**
- **diversity of experience**
- **understanding of the setting or medium**
- **ability and readiness to use information from elsewhere**
- **confidence and stamina to work beyond one's remit**

These ingredients are mutually supportive and reinforcing, as we discuss below. However, different features of public service organisations serve to limit the presence and strength of each of these ingredients, meaning that an active strategy is often required to overcome the obstacles to their development.

Curiosity

'Curiosity' is a readiness to question assumptions, established policies and ways of working. This curiosity may result in a deliberate decision to re-assess approaches to a problem. It is also a way of thinking that allows new ideas to surface, even without a conscious decision to re-assess. Curiosity means that the exploration of new possibilities is wide ranging, allowing the development of new perspectives on problems and new interpretations of what causes them.

Curiosity was in play when Greater Manchester Police decided to re-assess their approach to night-time disorder and appointed two people to re-examine the underlying causes of the growth in crime and violence and to develop a new approach based on their analysis. Project 218 in Glasgow was also the result of a re-think of traditional practice. There was a recognition at Ministerial level and elsewhere of the inappropriateness of existing court sentences for the increasing numbers of women offenders in Scotland, most of whom posed little harm to others.

The result of curiosity is often an explanation of a problem, and an answer to it, that encompasses a much wider context than in previous thinking. This depends on the people involved understanding more than their particular field or specialism and seeing a situation from a perspective other than their own professional or occupational stance. Thus, curiosity is nourished by a diversity of experience and is often associated with a readiness to use information from elsewhere.

In George's Mental Health Trust, for example, key people not only focused on the needs of their service users or client groups but were also able to understand and address the needs of NHS organisations as employers to fill important vacancies and skills gaps. Awareness of the needs of different groups, and seeing a situation from another perspective, were also evident in the aviation case study. There, the aviation enthusiasts understood the concerns of the security services at the airport and were able to suggest an approach that could meet the needs of both groups.

While the case studies showed that curiosity is sparked by the need to solve a particular problem and to find a new way of achieving desired outcomes, this curiosity can also be stifled by the need to meet specific deadlines. Pressure to meet targets can limit people's time and energy to think about different approaches, especially approaches that need time to develop, implement and show results. Their attention becomes focused on doing more of the same, rather than on inventing something different.

Even where pressure is not intense, curiosity may not flourish. A highly prescriptive style of directing organisations or of managing people and performance can encourage staff to think that problem-solving is someone else's responsibility. A strongly conservative attitude, which may stem from discomfort at the possibility of change, or anxiety about its possible results, can also stifle curiosity.

The motivation to do better

We can identify two levels of motivation that are a necessary component of creativity.

Firstly, there is a strong underlying motivation in public services that is often referred to as the public service ethos.[19] People are motivated in their work by the desire to produce public value – to deliver effective services, to increase user satisfaction and, broadly speaking, to 'make a difference' for service users and the community. This underlying motivation is necessary if people are to search for better ways of meeting public needs and demands.

Secondly, people are motivated to deal with specific problems or issues. A strong interest and concern for a particular issue leads people to focus their attention and energy upon it. Often this is driven by a strong personal conviction on the part of the people concerned that better outcomes are necessary and possible in their area of particular interest.

In some of the case studies, a strong belief in the central importance of the services for service users' quality of life was a particularly important motivation. For example, innovation in the school meals service was driven by a strong conviction that the quality of food matters to children's welfare. The Urban Village initiative was driven by the belief that homeless people need more than accommodation if they are to shape better lives for themselves.

Despite the strong underlying motivation to produce public value, the urgency of achieving immediate objectives can mean that the possibility of developing new and more effective approaches is all but forgotten. It is for this reason that we find that creative ideas often develop where people have a very strong interest in a particular issue, which can prevail even in the face of other pressures.

A long-term vision of better outcomes

Clarity about objectives and intended outcomes is a key component of creativity, which involves looking beyond the more immediate concerns of organisations with their short-term performance targets. It is important in motivating people because it provides them with a shared understanding of what they are trying to achieve and thus a context for exercising their curiosity and drawing on diverse experiences.

The focus on how to achieve outcomes, rather than outputs, involves understanding the impact of different actions and can be a basis for using information from elsewhere and for exploring alternative methods of achieving the desirable results. A longer-term vision allows the time for an innovation to take effect and for outcomes to become evident.

Several of the case studies recognised that their creative ideas, which were directed at achieving a sustainable improvement in outcomes, would take some time to bear fruit. The Urban Village initiative, for example, set out to improve the quality of life for homeless people by helping them to greater independence, rather than just to reduce rough sleeping by providing hostel places.

Project 218 in Glasgow set out to improve the longer-term prospects for women offenders, thereby reducing re-offending, rather than to punish them with imprisonment. And police community support officers developed from a search for an alternative to increasing the police presence in public places, in order to find sustainable and cost-effective response to the need for increased security.

These case studies had long-term visions on which to draw in developing their ideas. It is important that public service organisations develop and communicate such visions, and maintain them during organisational change. People who work in public services are used to frequent change in organisational structures, policy, and political and management priorities. However, where such change is frequent or extensive, it absorbs energy and causes enough disruption to distract people's attention from their overall purpose. It becomes difficult to maintain a longer-term and overall vision of what an organisation is trying to achieve, and to communicate this consistently and regularly. Without a longer-term vision, people are more likely to continue with their current ways of working, especially if these seem to be serving the short-term objectives more or less satisfactorily.

Diversity of experience

A range of different experiences came together in each case study. Protagonists in almost all of them were in touch with networks beyond the usual ones for people in their positions and had a variety of personal experiences, including those from previous jobs. This diversity of experience brought a range of knowledge and perspectives that greatly facilitated the re-interpretation or re-analysis of a problem, the vision of outcomes and the understanding of how these might be achieved.

In some cases individuals bring different experiences or perspectives to a situation and can act as a catalyst for new thinking, even if this was not the intention. In the case of NHS Direct, for example, an official had previously been involved elsewhere in looking at possible uses of new technologies. When he became involved at the early stage of thinking about new service ideas, which led to NHS Direct, he was able to contribute his previously acquired knowledge of these technologies. These were central to the developing vision of an innovative telephone-based service.

In other cases, there is a deliberate attempt to draw together different experiences in a way that might feed the development of new ideas. The Camden Boulevard project set out deliberately to blur boundaries in a traditional, compartmentalised organisation. It brought people together from different service areas to share ideas, look for new connections and develop new approaches.

For various reasons, a diversity of experience is not always easily available in public services. Many people's working lives are limited to a single type of organisation, function or profession. The much-discussed tendency for public services to work in departmental or functional 'silos' prevents the 'joining-up' of experience to create new solutions to common problems. Specialised jobs and responsibilities, especially if these also bring heavy workloads, limit the opportunities to come into contact with other experiences. Heavy workloads may also create a desire to limit one's contact with a diversity of experiences, in order to make one's job manageable.

Understanding of the setting or medium

In the case studies the imaginative thinking was done mainly by people close to the place where the resulting innovation would eventually be implemented. It was thinking by people who know their field well, and who understand the problems and why the current approach is not working. Their understanding is a foundation for exploring possibilities in a way that will lead to useful results.

The support or involvement of senior people is required to take this imaginative thinking forward into the implementation of an innovation, but it is often the people closest to the problem who are responsible for the initial ideas. Research by Borins in the USA concluded that half (51 per cent) of all innovations in the public sector originated with either middle managers or front-line staff.[20] Not everyone will want to develop new ideas but the chance of their doing so is increased if they are encouraged to reflect on ways to improve current practice and if they are confident that their suggestions will be heard and considered.

Senior people in public services need to be careful about bringing in 'outsiders' with a fresh perspective on established problems. While this can be helpful, particularly if it increases the diversity of experience, it can alienate the support of insiders, especially if they see wheels being re-invented or feel that they would have proposed the new solution themselves, had they been given the opportunity.

The importance of the detailed knowledge and understanding held by staff at the 'front line' of a problem was evident in the case studies. For example, much of the initial thinking behind the radical changes to the school meals service was done by the catering managers, who were passionate about school food and also had knowledge of the catering sector and the local farm and food economy. Similarly, the New Ways of Working initiatives were developed with the staff who would be closely involved and directly affected by the new working arrangements.

Very senior people were involved in the creative thinking behind the innovations that are largest in scale and highest in profile. Possibly these are the only people with the necessary overview and understanding of the 'whole system' to develop some initial ideas. For example, much of the initial thinking that led to the introduction of police community support officers is attributed to the then deputy commissioner of the Metropolitan Police. However, this and other case studies also had the involvement of other people throughout the creative process. These people were much closer to the point at which the problems that were being tackled were directly experienced. In the case of the PCSOs, a project team, comprising officers with a range of experiences and expertise, went on to develop the thinking.

Ability and readiness to use information from elsewhere

The thinking in the case studies was informed by scanning information and identifying developments outside people's immediate field of responsibility. This is a reflection of the curiosity that has already been mentioned as an ingredient of creativity. Thinking was also informed by formal arrangements for evaluation and analysis of the services under scrutiny. This helped to provide the necessary understanding of the field, which is another ingredient of creativity.

In all cases, this information sparked the imagination and helped to build new ideas that were tailored to the specific problem and its solution. The result was an original idea that was 'owned' by the protagonists. In some cases, physical contact with the places and people doing related work in other contexts can be helpful. Both the Camden Boulevard project and the St George's Mental Health Trust initiative had drawn on the experience of study visits abroad to explore alternative approaches to similar problems. The Urban Village initiative draws on a related project in New York. NHS Direct and Project 218 both reviewed evidence, including research and evaluations, from elsewhere about 'what works' as part of developing new thinking.

Organisations, or parts of them, have different cultures of information use. Where there is no expectation of evaluation or of drawing on information from experience elsewhere, the stimuli for new thinking are reduced. People may also perceive suggestions about doing things differently as criticism of their efforts.

Confidence and stamina to act beyond one's remit

Creativity, by our definition, involves imagination and, sometimes, 'thinking the unthinkable'. A degree of personal confidence and stamina is needed to put forward new ideas that may be controversial or provoke scepticism, criticism or even hostility from others. A long-term vision can be very helpful in giving people the confidence to promote new ideas that would serve the overall purpose of the organisation, even if they are unconventional in terms of current ways of working.

There is a crucial element of self-belief that separates the people who keep their ideas to themselves or stick with 'traditional' ways of working, from those who are willing to resist conformity and put forward suggestions for change to colleagues. For example, those developing the plans for police community support officers had to work hard to convince the Police Federation that PCSOs would assist policing and not undermine the role or effectiveness of police officers.

8 The creative process

We have defined creativity as the process of developing original ideas that have value. For the ideas and thinking to emerge and to begin to develop, the essential ingredients of creativity, discussed in the previous chapter, have to be present. However, this alone is not enough. In none of our case studies did the original ideas come quickly or already complete into being, but were developed through what was sometimes quite a lengthy process.

Here we analyse the process by which an idea was developed over time into a fully developed initiative or plan that is ready for implementation, with sufficient resources and appropriate support to allow implementation to begin. We examine the actions, skills and behaviours involved to bring the creative process to this end result.

The creative process comprises the following stages:
- **The giving or taking of time and space to think**
- **Getting support for developing ideas**
- **Shaping and re-shaping the ideas, in collaboration with others**
- **Championing the ideas to different agendas**
- **Holding to the essentials of the idea**
- **Getting support for implementing the proposals**.

It was rarely possible to identify a single individual who was responsible for an idea. And even where one person had played a large part in the initial thinking, others had also been involved in its development. Creativity in public services is a collaborative process. It is a social process as much as a formal or organisational one, but it requires the active input of managers and senior staff to ensure the process is initiated and completed.

The active support and management of this process also refreshes the supply of the essential ingredients of creativity, which were discussed in the previous chapter. For example, if people see new ideas being taken forward, their curiosity and motivation will be reinforced. Where they see an absence of senior support for developing ideas, people will lose the confidence and stamina to make unconventional proposals.

The giving or taking of time and space to think

In busy working lives people need time and space to think about alternative ways of doing things, to reflect and to learn, to develop ideas and perhaps to experiment. Some people, aware of the germs of an idea, will carve out the time to develop it further. In some cases, heavy workloads can trigger the determination to find an alternative way of working.

More commonly, the pressure to meet short-term objectives can make it difficult to find the time to think about different approaches, especially as people in some jobs have little or no control over their own workloads. The beginnings of a potentially successful innovation can be ignored or forgotten if there is no opportunity to think further about the idea. Success in this stage of the process therefore requires managers to recognise the need for time and space to take preliminary ideas further, and to make this available where it's needed.

The importance of this is evident in the office of the Boulevard project in the London Borough of Camden, where the walls are covered with posters and quotations encouraging staff to think creatively, thereby giving a strong sense that they have the permission to take the time do so. The New Ways of Working programme provided a vehicle and an opportunity for thinking about developing new approaches to the organisation of functions and services. In both the Manchester City Centre Safe Project and Project 218 in Glasgow people were given time and a specific brief to re-think an approach to a problem.

Getting support for developing ideas

People with a conviction about the importance of finding a new approach to a problem and an attachment to the value of the developing ideas are often willing to put a great deal of energy and effort into getting the support they need to develop it further. However, they may lack opportunities to have contact with those whose support is needed, particularly if these are people who are more senior to them or in a different part of the organisation. They also need to be able to present their ideas in a way that will persuade those whose support is needed.

Success at this stage of the process therefore depends on the extent to which managers are receptive to staff making new suggestions that are at a very early stage of development. This stage of the process may run more smoothly where senior people have taken the lead in recognising the need for a new approach. However, relying on senior people as a source of ideas will deprive the organisation of the creativity of the majority of its people. An important role for senior people is to be receptive to new ideas and to support their development.

Where this support is not available, ideas may be lost. For example, the aviation enthusiasts' approach to the police could easily have been dismissed or ignored. Instead, senior people within the police service were open to the suggestion that improved cooperation with enthusiasts could lead to a mutually beneficial solution. And in both of the school meals projects the catering managers had support, from the earliest stages, of headteachers and school governors.

Shaping and re-shaping ideas

The process involves assessing ideas, developing them in a more detailed form, perhaps rejecting some elements and re-shaping others. The exchange of experiences from different settings and different networks helps to make connections between previously unconnected ideas and to spark new thinking. Recognition of the absolute boundaries to what might be possible and acceptable provides a structure for the thinking.

The scrutiny of ideas from a variety of perspectives helps to shape and inform the thinking. The input of people with different roles in an organisation, from the strategic to the front-line, is important. Challenge by sceptics or traditionalists can be especially useful as their objections can trigger new thinking about how to overcome obstacles.

This process of shaping ideas is helped by certain types of organisational structure: multi-layered or strongly compartmentalised structures make engagement with people in other parts of the organisation more difficult, as do very specialised jobs. This process also requires facilitation to maintain people's energy and enthusiasm.

This process of collaboration and scrutiny is evident in the case studies. For example, the development of the detailed proposals for Project 218, police community support officers and NHS Direct were all the result if bringing together people with different skills, knowledge and experiences to build on the original, preliminary ideas. The Urban Village also illustrates the need to shape and re-shape ideas. It is the second version of the plans for this project; original plans were reshaped to fit a UK context and the specific locality for the project.

Championing the ideas to different agendas

To get taken forward, most new ideas have to appeal to a number of people with different interests. It is necessary to understand the different agendas and objectives of those whose support or involvement is needed and to offer them a solution that is persuasive. This often requires dealing with opposition and resistance from those with vested interests or those who feel threatened by the prospect of change.

Potentially valuable ideas can be lost at this stage if the protagonists do not know what other people's agendas are, if they do not have access to senior people who need to be persuaded, or they lack the skill or authority to counter the unjustified rejection of ideas. The support of senior champions in advocating ideas can be critical, especially where a large number of people in different positions have to be persuaded.

Examples of this amongst the case studies include NHS Direct, which was designed to meet a range of different interests and could be advocated to different groups in different ways. The potential benefits included: for government and the public, improved and cost-effective access for the public to health information; for medical professions, a way of containing demand for out of hours GP services and accident and emergency services; and for nurses, new professional and employment opportunities.

Holding to the essentials of the idea

As ideas develop and get discussed by those whose involvement and support is needed, there can be two types of reaction that can threaten the originality of the ideas and their value. Firstly, the creative process may have to resist too much dilution of the original ideas by those with an interest in reverting to the more familiar or backtracking from radical change. Secondly, it may also have to protect an idea from over enthusiasm, for this may cause a rush towards implementation before the ideas have been fully developed, with potentially serious consequences.

Those involved in developing the ideas for implementation have to make difficult judgements between spending time in persuading doubters and pressing ahead to implementation. There may be a fine balance to be struck between spending time to refine an idea and moving quickly enough to build on the energy of the enthusiasts.

Initial resistance to the proposals for police community support officers was countered by making and maintaining a clear distinction was between their roles and responsibilities and those of police officers. This helped to make the proposal acceptable to the wider police service. In the case of NHS Direct, piloting the service in limited geographical areas allowed the service design to be refined before it was rolled out to the whole country. Evaluation reports helped to make the case for the service to be extended.

Getting support for implementing the proposals

Making the case for implementation is an integral part of the creative process. Giving life and shape to the ideas and the vision of what they could achieve requires the application of imagination. The more original or radical the ideas, the more important it is to have evidence from risk assessment exercises or piloting.

Even when such evidence is presented, there can be considerable resistance to innovation. Some of this may be genuine anxiety about the risk of unintended consequences such as a loss of service quality, user satisfaction or cost-effectiveness. In other cases resistance may be, overtly or otherwise, due to more personal or vested interests. Different tactics are required to deal with different types of resistance and get support for implementation.

Support for proposed innovations often has to be won, as at the St George's Mental Health Trust, where staff had to be convinced of the practicalities of training and employing service users as members of staff. The development of a well-structured training and support system for potential employees helped to convince existing staff of the potential benefits of the scheme and enabled its smooth implementation.

9 The creative climate: the role of leadership

Drawing on the experience of our interviewees and the literature review, we identify the distinctive things that leaders can do to encourage creativity. We do not seek to re-invent generic leadership skills here, but to analyse what needs to be done specifically to develop a 'climate' in which creativity can flourish. Leaders need not, and should not, feel responsible themselves for providing the creativity their organisations they need, but they can do a great deal to make it possible for there to be:

- a good supply of the essential ingredients of creativity in their organisations, and
- an environment in which the creative process is understood and supported.

The following leadership actions contribute to the development of a creative climate in public service organisations:

- **Leadership by example**
- **Valuing people and their ideas**
- **Providing a vision of the future**
- **Managing risk**
- **Delegating responsibility and giving freedom**
- **Developing external relationships.**

Leadership by example

People throughout public services encourage creativity through their leadership, although those at the top, in governance and senior executive roles, have particular responsibilities. Their actions send a signal about the kind of behaviour that is needed and can strongly influence attitudes and motivation throughout the organisation.

Leaders can lead by example by demonstrating their own curiosity about the causes of problems and about alternative approaches. By being ready to question assumptions overtly, they encourage others to step outside the 'comfort zone' of familiar ways of working. By maintaining a focus on outcomes and service improvement, they encourage others not to settle for the status quo when better alternatives might be created.

Leaders also carry the greatest accountability for decisions to implement innovations, so must exemplify an active approach to risk management, which supports innovation.

Valuing people and their ideas

Putting forward new ideas, particularly any that are preliminary thoughts or are very unconventional, takes courage and conviction. This is much easier to do in an environment where 'nonconformist' views and ideas are actively encouraged and individuals are reassured that their ideas are valuable.[21][22] For leaders, this means encouraging and being willing to accept ideas from people anywhere in the organisational hierarchy, especially as creative thinking about problem-solving often comes from people closest to the problems.

If creativity is encouraged successfully, there may be more ideas originated than it is sensible to pursue. It may only be practical to move forward for serious consideration and development on a few, both because of the value of the ideas and because of the practicalities of putting resources into their development.[23] Senior staff usually have the role of providing the first screen or filter for these ideas. They must make careful judgements, alert to the possibility of dismissing a potentially useful idea by being too cautious or conservative or because it does not obviously fit with existing strategies.

Celebrating the success of even small innovations encourages a positive attitude to developing new ideas. Recognising the value of useful failure can limit the damage caused to the innovation 'mindset' caused by any recent experience of failed initiatives.[24]

Creativity requires a diversity of people, of experiences and interactions. Living Innovation, the Department for Trade and Industry initiative to encourage innovation in business, notes that creative teams have networks that extend beyond the internal workforce, drawing on the experience of different links in the service delivery chain, including partner organisations and service users.[25] A creative climate can be fostered by encouraging individuals to develop their networks and by making time for discussions that encompass both operational and policy staff within organisations.

Building the capacity of team members to suspend assumptions and genuinely think together is part of becoming a 'learning organisation' that fosters creativity.[26] However, simply bringing a diverse group together in order to 'brainstorm' may not generate creativity . Group members may be defensive or competitive, engaging in 'turf wars'. Leaders have to help groups to build a sense of shared purpose, and therefore a reason to make the most of their differences.[27][28]

An organisational culture that places a high premium on exercising initiative and striving for continual improvement will also encourage creativity. Leadership for creativity will seek to incorporate these values into organisational systems and processes so that employees adopt them as part of their approach to working and are aware of the possibilities for change.[29]

Providing a vision of the future

Creativity is aided by a clear and consistent vision of what an organisation is trying to achieve in the medium-term, and by allowing innovations the time to make a difference. This runs counter to the short-term budgetary and planning horizons that often prevail in public services, and which require quick returns. A comparison of public and private sectors noted that few innovative businesses would survive an obligation to break even every year, and that requirements for two or three per cent efficiency gains per annum encourage less innovation than seeking a twenty per cent improvement over five years.[30]

Managing risk

People running public services are held to account for the results of their actions. This accountability of public servants for the human, social and financial results of their decisions instils in them a necessary caution, but the same caution can also hold back the creativity that is needed. The National Audit Office suggested that government departments were 'more risk averse than risk taking' and noted that government departments tended to focus on financial, project and compliance risks, rather than the risk of missing an opportunity.[31] [32] [33]

Leaders need to make sure that their organisations have well developed risk assessment and risk management skills and systems and these are operating effectively. Such organisations are more likely to be in a position to be creative[34]. They can take better informed decisions about the implementation of innovation, because they understand the risks involved and have worked out how to minimise them. This can counteract the anxiety involved in trying new things.

Delegating responsibility and giving freedom

Appropriate devolution of responsibility can provide individuals with the incentive and permission to approach tasks and problems in new and creative ways, and strengthen their motivation to improve outcomes and service quality. Research for the Industrial Society suggests that working more creatively is likely to require less hierarchical structures, and new patterns of work that don't necessarily conform to the traditional '9 to 5' or to narrowly defined roles and rules[35]. The DTI identifies trust and respect between senior managers and staff as a key motivator, creating a flexible framework and structure in which people are free to get on with the job and give their best.[36]

New thinking emerges when middle managers have the skills, capacity and initiative to take action on their own accord, and service providers have the energy and imagination to respond to different service users' particular needs.[37] People need to be encouraged to think for themselves and to take responsibility for their roles, within a framework of support and accountability.

This can be a challenge for traditional views of management and efficiency. Senior levels of the organisation will need to cede some of their control to managers further down the hierarchy, and to manage their own fear of losing control.

Developing external relationships

People in public services are accountable to many others outside the organisation – to the public as well as to partners, inspectors and regulators, central government and parliament, and so on. Real accountability requires a dialogue as well as the giving of a report on actions already completed. This dialogue is an opportunity to build mutual understanding and trust and thus to increase the likelihood of the necessary external support for innovation. Leaders are important in fostering strong relationships with stakeholders outside the organisation.

This dialogue is particularly important when public services deal with 'wicked' problems, which demand creativity. It is difficult to test the potential impact of any proposed innovation in wicked problem areas on the public and service users. By developing a dialogue with their stakeholders, public services have the opportunity to test and re-shape ideas as they work towards implementation. Over time, open and communicative relationships with other agencies and partners help to stimulate thinking and provide constructive challenge for new ideas. They also establish the climate that will encourage support for any proposed innovations that require inter-agency co-operation.

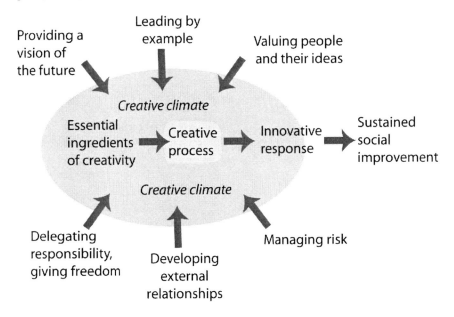

10 Conclusions

As members of the public and as service users, we all need creativity in public services. People working in creative public services are not necessarily satisfied with traditional ways of doing things. They develop approaches that enable better performance in familiar situations and they respond smartly to changes in the society they serve. Faced with new challenges, creative public services develop new ideas to apply to often-complex problems, leading to improved social outcomes and the more effective use of limited resources.

Yet evidence of this 'home-grown' creativity in public service organisations is not plentiful. Of course, policy changes and new ways of working are introduced in public services all the time. However, most of these are changes that outside authorities (central government or regulators, for example) require organisations to implement, or are adoptions or slight adaptations of innovations already implemented elsewhere. This means that public service organisations are denying the public and themselves the benefits of their own potential for creativity – their potential to respond imaginatively to the specific situations they find themselves in and to develop ideas that might also go on to be of value to the wider public and other organisations.

We can be confident that there exists the potential, as well as the need, for more creativity in public services. The potential comes, first, from the motivation of people working in public service organisations. The majority of them are there because they value public services and want to help to provide the public with a better service.

Second, public service organisations have proven their ability to initiate and implement innovations in their own work, bringing significant and sustained benefits to the public. We know that public services can be creative as part of their own search for improvement, as well as in response to crises, new technologies or incentives offered by external agencies.

Third, creativity in public services is a collaborative process, not the product of isolated or atypical mavericks, and much can be done to foster this collaboration. Public services are well-placed to make connections between people from top to bottom, from the centre to the front-line of organisations, and with service users, citizens and partners. They can make connections between all the people who bring different perspectives and experiences of what needs to change.

How can public services make more of this potential? To do so requires an active strategy, which will unlock the potential of people throughout the organisation to be creative. It means taking steps to give creativity the best chance of flourishing and of contributing to sustained social improvement. Without such a strategy creativity is at best sporadic, and less likely to bear fruit in the form of useful innovation. Sustained creativity is not a matter of luck or accident but requires an explicit strategy. While many public service organisations and public service leaders acknowledge the importance of creativity, few have pursued a strategy that pays attention, simultaneously, to all four components of creativity in public services:

- being alert to opportunities for creative change (see chapter 6)
- ensuring that the essential ingredients for creativity are in place (see chapter 7)
- supporting and managing the creative process (see chapter 8)
- providing leadership to develop a climate for creativity inside an organisation and it its external relations (see chapter 9).

While creativity cannot be prescribed, a comprehensive strategy, based on all of these components, can provide the right conditions for creativity to flourish. Further, the strategy has to reinforce, and be reinforced by, other important strategies and systems in the organisation or sector. These systems influence, for example, the priority given to creative problem-solving and establish different motivations and incentives to be creative, or not. Without this lining up of strategies and systems, efforts to encourage creativity can be frustrated.

Among these strategies and systems, those for human resources are particularly important. Systems of appraisal and reward should recognise the value of ideas (including unsuccessful ones), of a focus on improving outcomes, and of leadership for creativity. Approaches to recruitment should bring in a diverse range of people who share the organisation's commitment to better outcomes, who bring new ideas and fresh thinking, and who increase the variety of experiences and backgrounds in the staff team.

Staff development policies can increase the diversity of experience and stimulate thinking by giving people experience outside the organisation and beyond the mainstream activities of their jobs. This development of people's knowledge and understanding is reinforced in an organisation that values learning, evaluation and knowledge management. Creative ideas emerge where people have an in-depth understanding of their fields and wide-ranging knowledge of related areas.

None of this is going to happen if people do not have time to think and develop new ideas. If they are consumed by short-term targets, or feel they have no control over deadlines, workload or the approach they are required to take, they are unlikely to have the time and space to be creative. Public service organisations need to take the bold step of focusing energy on delivering today's solutions while at the same time making the space for their people to create tomorrow's.

Appendix A: Case studies

Aviation Enthusiasts' ID Card

Introduction

The creative idea in this case study came from a member of the public, in response to a crisis in his particular field of interest. The underlying objective was to improve relationships between a section of the public and the police, to mutual benefit. We selected it as an example of a very simple idea's potential to make a positive impact on a national, and indeed international, scale.

The problem

The threat of terrorism in the UK saw a significant increase in airport security in the wake of 11 September 2001. Viewing platforms were closed at several airports, including Heathrow, on the advice of the Home Office. Aviation enthusiasts reported a more hostile attitude from police officers, who were much more inclined to view their activities with suspicion and move them on from viewing areas.

The idea

In early 2003, David Seex, the chair of one of the largest aviation enthusiast clubs, LAAS International, wrote to the Commissioner of the Metropolitan Police, and suggested that the police and enthusiasts find ways to work together to reduce hostility and tackle crime and terrorism. He noted that at most airports there were usually more enthusiasts than police, and proposed enlisting the help of enthusiasts to be the 'eyes and ears' of the police on the ground.

The innovation

The Aviation Enthusiasts' Security Scheme aims to encourage enthusiasts to use their experience and knowledge of aviation to report suspicious activity, and to take a responsible approach in their activities at airports. The scheme also aims to persuade airport authorities and police officers that enthusiasts have a positive role to play in the fight against crime and terrorism, and to improve relations between police and enthusiasts.

How it happened

Aviation Security, represented by the Chief Inspector of the Heathrow police service, was tasked with making contact with LAAS to take the idea further. Heathrow, as the UK's largest airport, provided the pilot for a scheme. Heathrow police had already identified enthusiasts as a core group at the airport, together with airport and airline staff, with whom it wished to develop contacts and encourage cooperation.

The Police, British Airports Authority and LAAS collaborated to develop an ID card for enthusiasts. Membership of the scheme requires signing up to a code of conduct, which commits enthusiasts to reporting unusual activity as well as keeping away from security fences. The card includes information on what to look out for and who to contact in the event of suspicious behaviour. It also aims to help airport operators 'identify the real, responsible enthusiasts.' LAAS operates the scheme, which is open to all enthusiasts.

Challenges

Past incidences of hostility between police and enthusiasts have created negative perceptions on either side. Police and airport staff needed some convincing. The code of conduct aimed to address this issue. Staff had to be reassured that the enthusiasts would not perceive the card as granting them any special leave to enter restricted areas, and that membership criteria would be robust.

Some enthusiasts were suspicious of the scheme. Police have had to reassure them about the voluntary nature of the scheme and sell this as their chance to act against crime and terrorism and support their hobby by ensuring that a high standard of behaviour is maintained.

The scheme does not involve police checking of members. To manage the potential risks to the police it was agreed that LAAS would operate and take responsibility for the scheme, while the police would endorse it and promote awareness. There has been a big publicity and awareness raising campaign, but briefing of police forces and guards around the country will need to continue on a long-term basis. Awareness of the scheme is improving but it will take some time to convince both staff and enthusiasts of the benefits.

What helped

The police recognised LAAS as a serious player, and discussions took off relatively quickly. Both parties recognised the mutual benefits of finding ways to accommodate one another's priorities.

The chair of LAAS and the Chief Inspector of Heathrow Police, as representative of Aviation Security, established a close working relationship with regular contact. The police and BAA (British Airports Authority) recognised the benefits of the idea and supported it. Having secured endorsement from the authorities LAAS was able to take on the administration of the scheme. The membership fee alleviates the need for the public sector to carry any cost. The risks involved in developing the scheme were not significant. Robust membership criteria and the ability of enthusiasts to identify interlopers limit the extent to which the scheme could be abused.

Impact and issues

The scheme was formally launched in May 2004. There are now approximately 1000 members and the number continues to grow. Following testing at Heathrow, the card has been rolled out on a national level. All police services with airports within their remit are aware of the scheme, and police have improved their contacts with this community. LAAS and the police perceive the scheme as being in a very early stage that will continue to evolve and gain momentum.

The scheme has generated huge media interest. Appropriate handling of this interest has been crucial to the success of the project.

Anecdotal evidence suggests that officers tend to treat card-carrying enthusiasts with more respect, and are less hostile and intrusive. There has been a decrease in incidents of enthusiasts using illegal means to gain access to viewing sites. LAAS has received positive feedback from members.

Aviation security is improving its communications systems to allow it to be more responsive to the information it receives from airport staff and enthusiasts. People are able to email their concerns to the station, and control staff filter emails to ensure that urgent messages are picked up immediately.

BAA note that, since the introduction of the scheme, Heathrow is even more committed to taking a coordinated approach to tackling crime and terrorism, working with other key stakeholders. Contacts are now in place to make connections, and new ways of engaging with different communities, such as taxi drivers, are being explored.

The Camden Boulevard Project

Introduction

This local authority initiative arose as a way of improving and maintaining good levels of service, while recognising the need to do something very different to convince members of the public of the quality of the service. Camden Council recognised that individual services were operating effectively, so it shifted its focus to improving links between them. The risks were significant: a lot of money needed to be invested in an untried initiative in order for it to work; and people would be asked to blur boundaries in what had traditionally been a fairly 'silo'-based organisation. We selected this as a useful example of how a creative approach can be used to encourage more effective ways of working with minimal disruption to existing structures.

The problem

Camden Council sought to achieve a 'quantum leap' in performance in its street-scene activities. Customer satisfaction surveys showed a perception gap between what the public thought of environmental services, and how the council perceived itself as performing. Senior managers recognised that maintaining forward momentum required a willingness to try new approaches.

The idea

The existing structure was functioning effectively. However, the interface between services could potentially be improved. The Boulevard Project was set up as an overarching unit, tasked with identifying gaps in service and rethinking how different service areas could work more effectively together.

The innovation

The Boulevard Project brings people together from different service areas and from outside the council to share ideas, look for new connections and approach problems in new ways. The overall objective is to generate the most attractive streets in Europe.

How it happened

The Council leader and chief executive had recently returned from a fact-finding visit to various North American cities aimed at gathering ideas and good practice. Senior managers recognised that the service, while close to top performers across the country, had to keep the forward momentum, which required doing something very different rather than continuing to try to make incremental improvements. The Project was set up with the intention of finding innovative ways to move things forward. A strategic change manager was appointed to head the service, supported by an administrative assistant, PR officer and community engagement officer. The council is spending about £24 million over five years. The money comes from the council's budget for building, roads and other major physical projects.

Challenges

Initially, politicians required considerable persuasion before they were convinced of the returns on investment, given that the approach had not been tried before and significant funding was required to make the project work.

People were being asked to blur responsibilities and boundaries and this was sometimes perceived as threatening. It was important to keep talking to people and explaining the thinking behind the initiative. People have to be persuaded to identify with the Boulevard brand, rather than with their particular service areas. A lot of effort needs to go in to building the project's reputation – Boulevard's remit requires that the team put in a lot of time building their visibility and ensuring that they are recognised as approachable and credible among all partner groups. Much time needs to be spent building the reputation of the programme, publicising successes and building relationships.

What helped

The project has had strong political support from the Council, which recognised the need to do something different and innovative to improve public perceptions. The change manager appointed to head the service is enthusiastic about and committed to finding creative ways to make improvements. The project has its own budget, which allows the manager flexibility to allocate resources when people from different departments approach him with good ideas, without having to go through a long bureaucratic process. People know that their ideas will get a fair listening.

Impact and issues

The project has succeeded in establishing itself as a recognised brand. Customer surveys show that satisfaction after a major Boulevard intervention is up to 80 per cent. Within the council, the project has demonstrated the value of thematic working, challenging the traditional silo approach. Key issues for the project are how to better align public perceptions and the reality of performance regarding the street scene, and how to keep improving and building on good work.

Camden Boulevard Community Grants Scheme

Introduction

The Community Grant Scheme was developed through collaboration between a voluntary sector agency and local council. The scheme was an entirely new initiative, and provided an opportunity for both the council and the agency to improve and expand their existing service for the benefit of local people. The allocation of funding to community groups might have seemed a considerable risk, but was managed through a range of controls and support mechanisms built into the approach. We selected this scheme as an example of a creative mechanism to enable local communities to take responsibility for their local environment, and indication of the big impact that can be made by using small amounts of funding in creative ways.

The problem

Camden Boulevard was well established as a brand and was recognised as doing a lot of good work. Initially, however, the scheme had limited success in its efforts to engage local communities. At the same time, the Council recognised that there were a lot of small, niggling problems specific to particular areas that caused dissatisfaction for local residents but could not feasibly be addressed within the existing Council remit.

The idea

In 2001 Groundwork Camden and Islington[38] approached the council to discuss how it could best employ a £5 000 development grant, attached to SRB2 funding for 'Vital Centres.' Groundwork was already running several grant schemes and had an established track record and good relationships with the Council. Senior managers in the two organisations came up with a scheme that would allow small grants to be made direct to local community groups, to tackle specific small-scale issues within their particular area. The head of the Boulevard Project together with a senior manager at Groundwork were tasked with developing the details of the scheme.

The innovation

Boulevard project recognised the scheme's potential to address gaps that the council could not reach, and to boost its efforts to engage with local communities. The aim is to link local communities to the streetscape, encouraging people to take pride in their local environment and to share responsibility for its upkeep, 'creating a positive upward spiral.' The scheme allows community groups to bid for funding to undertake and manage small projects within their areas, for example planting a vacant plot of land with flowers to deter people dumping rubbish. Applicants commit their time and labour while the scheme provides tools, resources and permission to act. The Boulevard project provides the majority of funding for the scheme, with additional funding from Housing. There is £150 000 available for grants.

How it happened

Groundwork undertook a feasibility study, talking to a range of existing groups to find out what they would be interested in and their willingness to get involved and commit the necessary time and effort. This received good feedback. The SRB development grant provided the initial funding to implement a pilot, which ran in 2003, and proved successful. The scheme criteria were drawn up to be as wide as possible, while building in risk management in the form of minimum legal requirements that groups must comply with, access to support and guidance for groups throughout the process, comprehensive monitoring arrangements to ensure that funds are appropriately accounted for, and a careful panel-based selection procedure that includes the three partner agencies and community representatives.

Challenges

In 2003 the uptake was fairly low. The time lapse between the feasibility study and implementation was very short, and did not leave enough time for awareness raising.

Positive publicity has seen an impressive increase in the number of applications for subsequent rounds.

What helped

The collaboration provided the council with an effective route for community engagement. The Council and Groundwork had already established a good working relationship and were able to build on this trust. The existence of the Boulevard Project, with a remit to develop and support creative approaches to improving the street scene, suggested a sustainable source of funding for the scheme if it proved successful. Groundwork had good links with community groups, while association with the established Boulevard brand helped get the project off the ground. Availability of SRB funds for the initial pilot allowed Groundwork to demonstrate the feasibility of the scheme, and thus to secure Boulevard and subsequently Housing funding. Securing the involvement and support of the Camden Housing once the project was up and running helped to broaden the scope of the scheme to ensure relevance for local communities.

Impact and issues

The scheme offers applicants and awardees active outreach in the community setting, and is much more interactive and supportive than conventional grant schemes. Part of its intended effect is to empower and inspire others in the community.

The scheme has produced some imaginative ideas to resolve nagging issues. It has been very successful in reaching people that wouldn't normally apply for grants, including ethnic minority groups and elderly people. A large proportion of applications are received from very small groups and from areas of social housing.

The project brings home the message that the council is taking pride in the community, and encourages local people to do the same. The scheme is intended to be ongoing, as more people become aware of the possibilities and become involved. Boulevard Project aims to raise awareness of the scheme on a national scale later in 2005.

Healthy Eating in Schools

Note: Some information for this case study was drawn from the Soil Association's 'Food for Life: healthy, organic school meals' report, 2003. The initiatives in this case study predated the current move to healthier eating in schools, which has government backing in the wake of a 2005 TV series by Jamie Oliver.

Introduction

This case study concerns Blackawton Primary School, Devon and St Peter's Primary School, East Bridgford, Nottinghamshire

The problem

The two schools in this case study were experiencing similar levels of dissatisfaction with the existing food supplies. Much of the food being supplied by County Council contractors was low grade, processed and not as healthy as the schools would have liked.

In Blackawton Primary School in Devon the teachers, governors and parents had expressed unhappiness with the quality of food being served by the school. In addition, the low take-up of school meals by children meant that the school catering service was becoming less and less viable. The school was obliged to provide meals for seven of the school children. Only 13 additional children were eating meals catered for by the school out of a total number of 120 pupils.

In St Peter's Primary School in Nottinghamshire, the catering manager was dissatisfied by the supplies on offer. She wanted to be assured of the provenance of the food she was serving, to increase take-up of school meals.

The idea

In Blackawton School the governors and head teacher decided to bring in a new caterer who could provide better school meals and encourage more children to take up the school meal provision. The new catering manager was not prepared to use the existing school supplies and felt that by sourcing food from local suppliers independent of the Council's contractors she could meet the school's objectives.

In St Peter's Primary School the catering manager convinced the head teacher that the school would benefit from opting out of local authority catering arrangements. This would enable sourcing of better quality food, thereby improving take-up. It would allow an increase in the wages of the catering staff, and create an opportunity to take advantage of their skills; they were becoming de-skilled as a result of being confined to serving food that was largely processed and pre-prepared.

In both schools, the need to stay within existing food budgets in designing the new arrangements was critical.

The innovation

The innovation was to source food from local suppliers independent of the local authority. This had a number of additional benefits:

- The schools could be assured of the quality of food they were purchasing as they could check the supplies.
- There could be a greater emphasis on fresh produce as the catering managers could determine their own menus.
- In one school, there was a further mutual advantage for school and suppliers: the suppliers could sell their produce that needed to be eaten that day and the school could purchase it at lower cost.

- Suppliers could also help the catering managers think about how to vary the menu through using other, cheaper supplies, such as alternative cuts of meat, which they may have not been aware of.
- The schools were supporting local businesses that had been struggling due to rural economic decline and the more recent foot and mouth crisis. Both schools are in rural locations with a number of children from farming families who take a keen interest in food issues.
- The children were able to participate in designing their own menus and were more engaged with food education. In Blackawton School children can put forward suggestions for menus, and can choose which days to take school meals according to the pre-prepared weekly menus. In addition, children visit the farm that supplies the school as part of their food education. In St Peter's Primary School, a mobile bakery visited the school and the children have been learning how to grow organic vegetables.

How it happened

In both schools the catering managers were strongly supported by the head teacher and governors, and parents and children were involved in making changes to menus. The catering managers developed relationships with local suppliers, designed the menus and their presentation. In Blackawton School, for example, the food is presented as picnics for the children to eat outside in summer.

Challenges

The major challenge was in changing the habits of parents who were providing packed lunches for their children. This was overcome by involving parents in the process. At Blackawton School a tea was held for all the parents where they were invited to make suggestions, a questionnaire was sent out to identify children's food preferences, and the service was promoted in the school newsletter. At St Peter's School, the parents were invited to a tasting session and provided with nutritional information.

What helped

The passion of both catering managers to provide local, quality food at a low cost has been key in enabling this initiative to succeed.

At Blackawton the catering manager is strongly supported by two administrative staff who work closely with her in budgeting, raising invoices and other financial and administrative matters. This support has been invaluable in enabling her to get the idea up and running.

At St Peter's Primary School, the head teacher helped in developing financial projections. In order to encourage children to take up the school meals, there was a deliberate policy of sitting children who had packed lunches next to those eating school lunches.

Impact and issues

At both schools the service has turned out far better than anticipated. Both catering managers went on to support other, local schools to develop their own independent school meals service, and in the case of St Peter's Primary School the catering manager this has become a significant part of her work.

Within weeks of the changes being introduced, the number of children taking school meals at Blackawton School rose to 75 and the number of children taking school meals at St Peter's Primary School has risen from 115 to 180 (out of 220 pupils).

The schools have been the centre of much publicity. Prince Charles visited Blackawton School's local organic supplier and met the school children. Local businesses are also benefiting from increased publicity. There was some concern that costs would increase but this has not been the case. Any profit made from the school meals is invested into the kitchen in order to buy new equipment and improve the quality of food sourced.

The behaviour of children at meal times has vastly improved and, overall, meal times are much calmer. In St Peter's Primary School the scheme has been extended, with the school now providing meals for local senior citizens, whose meal service had become unviable. The senior citizens eat once a week at the school sitting amongst the children.

Manchester City Centre Safe

Introduction

This initiative arose in response to a crisis, a breakdown in law and order. It represents not so much a single idea, as a decision to go back to basics and rethink the causes of the problem, in order to isolate and treat these in a holistic manner. The creativity has been in identifying the key problems that needed to be addressed and finding ways to solve these, through sharing of information between different agencies, partnership working, and a public information campaign. The scheme involves a range of initiatives that vary in the investment and risk management required. The key to success has been to find simple but effective solutions and to coordinate efforts toward the overall objective.

The problem

Between 1997 and 1999 Manchester city centre saw an increase of 242 per cent in the capacity of licensed premises, and a 225 per cent increase in alcohol related violent crime. Manchester's reputation was poor, investment was declining and politicians were demanding that something be done. Among 18 to 25s, there was a growing perception of the 'normalisation' of drunken, aggressive behaviour. Night time violence was costing the police a great deal of money in overtime pay.

The idea

Greater Manchester Police (GMP) recruited two senior people with a remit to go back to the drawing board, to re-examine the causes of the current crisis, and to develop a fresh approach based on a fuller understanding of the underlying causes.

The innovation

The City Centre Safe initiative was launched in September 2000. It seeks to work with partners across all sectors. It now has about twenty components, each of which address key aspects of the night time economy. There are four main aims:
- To reduce the number of serious assaults and glass related injuries
- To work in partnership with the licensed trade to improve the management of licensed premises
- To promote the provision of safe drinking
- To reduce the perception of drunkenness, rowdiness and disorder in Manchester city centre.

How it happened

The new unit aimed to take an holistic approach to the problem of late night violence. They went back to basics and reviewed how people travelled into the city at night, how they drank, how they moved around over the course of an evening, and how they got home. Looking at all these issues, they sought ways to make the whole experience safer. The approach was supported by the city council. External funding was obtained to allow the police to take full control of the project.

The unit brought together a range of stakeholders to talk about the problems, and asked everyone present to say what their own organisations could do to help to take things forward.

Challenges

- Building trust – Efforts to introduce new initiatives met with lack of cooperation and resistance from the council and from parts of the police service. A strong sense of 'we've tried this before and it failed' had to be overcome. The police were unwilling to share information about crime figures with the council, owing to past criticism, and neither service was enthusiastic about extending roles in order to work more effectively in this area. Police headquarters had to be convinced of the advantages of an open and honest approach, whereby the police service would release its crime figures and admit the problems it was facing. This helped to identify specific areas that could be targeted for intervention.

What helped

- Win-win solutions – Changes had to be actively sold and people convinced of the advantages. Both change leaders had previous experience of the business sector, one in sales and the other in the drinks industry. This provided useful insight when it came to identifying the advantages of change for private sector stakeholders. The importance of working with other stakeholders to convince them of mutual benefits, rather than confronting or coercing them, has been crucial.
- Senior support – The scheme, and its holistic approach, was encouraged and supported by senior management within the police. There was also a strong incentive across the service to change the city's reputation and to make people safer.
- Partnership working – The scheme works in partnership with the City Council, education, health departments, local business, and a wide range of other agencies, including the drinks industry. It also works with Durham University and Salford University, and takes advice about alcohol issues from an international expert on alcohol and its effects.
- Community support – The scheme has targeted a number of government agencies and local pubs clubs, hotels and other businesses to become supporters of the initiative in a number of ways. A local car dealership has provided a vehicle, and other companies have provided advertising space and sponsored the bottle bins.
- Branding – The scheme has a strong, easily identified brand, owned by GMP, which is widely publicised. The logo has been carefully chosen – the police crest does not appear on any of the advertising or promotional material. The scheme targets the 18-25 age group, and it was felt that this would be better achieved if it were not perceived as being a 'police' initiative.

Impact and issues

The project has been successful in halting the rise in violent crime. The number of serious assaults in Manchester City Centre has fallen significantly in the past three years.

City Centre Safe has been recognised for its expertise. As part of the government's plans to spread good practice, the change leaders have spoken at various conferences, and now have formal consulting roles, regularly visiting other services across the UK to offer help and advice on issues relating to the night-time economy. The scheme has also received enquiries from Ireland, America and Australia.

Initiatives include:

- Matched funding – Bars and pubs in the Peter Street area, as part of their local area partnership, have banded together to pay for one police officer on Friday and Saturday nights. As matched funding, Manchester police provide a second officer, and have responsibility for the area. The initiative has been included in the recent white paper of licensing reform, and is likely to be repeated across the UK.
- Bottle bins – In order to deal with the problem of bottles becoming street weapons, the police introduced new bins designed to prevent discarded bottles being retrieved. The result has been a reduction in glass on the city's streets, and a drop in glass-injuries at A&E.
- By-law to limit glass inflicted injury – Research in A&E showed large numbers of people with glass-inflicted injuries, from street fights and falling on glass. GMP applied to the Home Office for a by-law to prevent drinking from glasses and bottles in the street. The initial application was rejected. GMP challenged the decision, and in a joint application with Merseyside police, presented the Home Office with a paper showing how people's safety was being compromised by current behaviour, together with CCTV footage demonstrating the limitations of the existing legal provisions. A direct appeal to the Home Secretary won his support for the changes. The requested by-law was introduced on a pilot basis in Manchester and Merseyside in September 2000, and a year later was rolled out on a national level.
- The Best Bar None Awards scheme was developed in partnership with statutory agencies and the alcohol industry. The aim is to incentivise operators of licensed premises to raise standards. The scheme establishes a set of standards for the management of licensed premises, giving accreditation to those who qualify, with the potential to obtain discounts on their normal insurance premiums. A mixed panel, comprising people from different agencies and stakeholder groups, selects award winners from all accredited premises. Awards are presented at a high profile ceremony. The Best Bar None scheme is now being rolled out nationally.

Night time transport

Introduction

One of several problems facing GMP was the need to get people out of the city centre and safely home after closing time. The solution seemed obvious – to provide a night bus service. However, creativity was needed in order to make the proposal attractive to the Council and the bus companies, to resource it, and to ensure that people would perceive it as accessible, safe and convenient and therefore use it in large numbers. By establishing a clear business case for the bus companies, the police were able to facilitate the inception of a profit-making, self-sustaining service.

The problem

Five years ago Manchester had no night transport system. Buses did not operate and taxis refused to come into the centre because of safety fears. Large crowds of people built up on the streets at the end of an evening, leading to fights and public safety problems.

The idea

The police looked at similar projects elsewhere and identified the key issues that were important to stakeholders. They also considered research undertaken by places such as Sheffield Hallam University and the University of Illinois on designing out crime. Their research clearly indicated that users wanted well lit, supervised waiting areas, reasonable pricing, a regular, convenient and trusted service, and a sense that they were safe and protected. Bus drivers, who risked assault, needed to feel secure and have appropriate back-up systems.

The innovation

A package was agreed with six local bus companies, whereby night routes include a minimum of six stops along major routes, and police provide a common level of support. Late night buses commenced in November 2001. Bus company staff, wearing yellow jackets, supervise each stop. They act as 'bus loaders,' filtering out drunk and aggressive passengers. Users are charged a fixed fee for all journeys.

How it happened

The police secured external funding for CCTV on the buses and at stops, and advised the companies on the location of the cameras to ensure that any evidence obtained in this way would be admissible in court. NRF funds were employed to fund police time in bus stops in the initial phase of the project. The police also set up a system of night communication, which has good buy-in from relevant stakeholders, and is monitored by a police officer. There is now a night-time transport steering group, which includes the police, buses and taxis.

Challenges

The Council insisted that night-time transport would be too expensive, and that there was not enough money to make the option attractive to bus companies. It also pointed out the fragmentation of the bus services, arguing that the lack of continuity would make the service unworkable. The bus companies argued that their drivers would be unsafe working night shifts.

What helped

There was a financial incentive for companies to expand into the night-time market, if the police could provide a secure operating environment. The police worked with the bus companies to find out more about those drivers that had been assaulted, with a view to learning more about communication and coping skills. They found that it tended to be a small group who were repeatedly assaulted, rather than a larger group suffering one-off assaults. The police suggested conflict management training, together with mechanisms to ensure drivers' safety.

Impact and issues

The project is now financially viable and is no longer subsidised. There have been few night-time incidents. The team recognised the need to work with what they had – and the result has been the creation of a sustainable, self-funding system. Up to 30 000 people use the service each weekend.

NHS New Ways of Working

Introduction

New Ways of Working was one of a number of self-managed teams within the NHS Modernisation Agency. It supported the delivery of major targets in the NHS Plan to improve access to, and the quality of, patient services. The aim of the team is to ensure there are sufficient numbers of appropriately trained, motivated staff working in the right locations.

The Frimley Park Hospital NHS Trust and the Newcastle, North Tyneside and Northumberland Mental Health NHS Trust projects involved changes to working patterns, which had an impact on existing teams and roles.

a) Frimley Park Hospital NHS Trust (now an NHS foundation trust)

The idea

There are three core strands to the Frimley Park Hospital NHS Trust project, which falls within the Working Time Directive (WTD) initiative. First is the recruitment of an additional night nurse practitioner and medical technical assistants (MTAs) to support the medical staff 'on-take' team.[39] The night nurse practitioner will lead for Medical Assessment Units (MAUs) during the night. Second is improving patient assessment times and the throughput of emergency referrals by installing a series of advanced 'point of care' (PoC) testing equipment (used in the main by MTAs) in A&E and MAU to give faster results and diagnosis. Third is rearranging doctors' rotas and thereby reducing the number of unsocial hours they work.

The hospital

Frimley Park Hospital is a medium sized acute hospital in the south east of England, serving a population of around 370,000. The hospital has a staff of around 3000 and an annual turnover of more than £120 million. It is one of the largest local employers, with more than 90 per cent of its doctors, nurses, technicians, scientists and support staff coming from the surrounding community. Frimley Park is a Ministry of Defence Hospital Unit (MDHU).

The project

The specialities being 'tested' under the WTD project are A&E and General Medicine. The project proposal was completed 4 days after the initial idea had received Department of Health approval to be worked-up in more detail. Risk management was a key aspect of the proposal. Frimley Park is a Ministry of Defence Hospital Unit (MDHU) and at the time of proposal writing, war with Iraq was imminent so the impact of losing some staff had to be considered and contingency and mitigation plans developed.

Factors contributing to success

The WTD project manager describes Frimley Park as a 'good, creative and innovative hospital'. It is also felt to have a 'Can Do Attitude' and thus able to respond quickly to change. This is due in part to a flat internal structure and an open culture. The Chief Executive takes a strategic view, allowing General Managers to work independently within the strategic framework. There is space for wide-ranging discussion amongst General Managers, in a morning meeting held once every two weeks, without agenda. Frimley Park is also 'financially sound' and this too is felt to have given those involved the freedom to think openly.

Good project management and a director-led Steering Group, which included external and internal project partners, ensured that the project remained on budget and on time. Support from key senior management staff was also important. The Director acted as a champion for the project both internally and externally. Senior nursing and pathology staff backed it inside the hospital.

An internal training programme for MTAs was also developed. External courses are available, but the hospital realised that it could provide its own training in a shorter time, allowing new staff to be join the workforce more quickly and to be used as locums.

The Night Nurse Practitioners work to a very high standard and are seen as providing additional support to some inexperienced Senior House Officers (SHO). They also ensure a tailored quality of service at the time of day when medical cover is at its lowest (in terms of individual doctors). Extensive surveys have shown the 'skills sets' needed for the 'night-time' coverage of patients and these have been included in the Night Nurse Practitioners Role and extended training.

A survey of patients and junior doctors provided positive feedback on the project. Night Nurse Practitioners were being used and valued and the MTAs were recognised as part of the team rather than 'add-ons'.

Issues and concerns

The project is not yet complete, so its impact cannot be fully assessed. No serious problems have been encountered to date. Issues that have arisen include:

Technical: The PoC equipment was new, untested and temperamental and the extent of its use was difficult to anticipate, so initially their use was a 'labour of love'. However, pathology staff recognised that the equipment would save them time in the long run, supported the MTAs and were prepared to accept the early teething problems.

Staffing: Some internal staff issues have been identified. Given the changes in roles and working practices, it was seen as inevitable that some staff would be unsettled and that there would be some professional rivalry and concern over professional status. These issues were managed by including potentially negative staff in the steering group from the start.

There is also concern that the NNPs will leave the hospital: their skills are much in demand throughout the NHS and in private medicine.

Cultural differences: The MTAs role was to provide support for MAU and A&E. The MTAs found it difficult within A&E to 'fit in' with an already established and consultant lead area of the Hospital. The MTAs, who are a hybrid role, were at one point in the project felt to be performing duties that were outside their remit and so the decision has been taken to take them out of A&E. This problem was not entirely unexpected: the previous experience of using MTAs had indicated that their role would need to be carefully managed. The MTAs have now been re-established at the same time as the introduction and wider use of more patient protocols.

b) Newcastle, North Tyneside and Northumberland Mental Health NHS Trust

The idea

The fundamental idea behind the project, which was developed by pharmacy staff at St George's Hospital in Morpeth, was to re-shape pharmaceutical services and other staff roles in the interests of developing a patient-focused service.

The hospital

St George's Hospital, Morpeth, houses the headquarters of the Newcastle, North Tyneside and Northumberland Mental Health NHS Trust. This is one of the largest mental health trusts in England, providing in-patient and community based mental health services across three localities: Newcastle upon Tyne, North Tyneside and Northumberland and integrated services for older people in Newcastle.

St George's Hospital provides adult acute in-patient services, including a Mother and Baby Unit, Occupational Therapy and Physiotherapy for in- and outpatients, and psychological assessment, therapy and consultation services for adults, both within the hospital and in community settings. Psychological Services also leads research and development for the Northumberland locality of the trust.

These services will shortly be re-housed in new facilities on the same grounds. The new hospital will have 203 beds. Small on-site houses with their own bedrooms and bathrooms will be available for patients needing longer-term care.

The project

The project focused on the roles of the pharmacy staff. The roles of pharmacists and pharmacy technicians were re-defined and the new role of Dispensing Assistant (ATO) was introduced. Pharmacy services were centred on the ward, rather than being remote from patients, in the dispensary. Pharmacy staff became part of the wider patient care teams.

The project would provide patients with a seamless pharmacy service, from admission through to discharge. Medication summaries, including a history, were taken on admission. Patients' own drugs could be used once assessed for suitability, so helping to reduce costs for the hospital and allowing the potential for increased patient compliance with their prescribed treatment. Proactive pharmacy input resulted in the reduction in any delay for patients receiving their medicines.

The existing pharmacy service at St George's Hospital had been in place for 20 years. Pharmacy staff identified a range of problems with the service, including poor risk management, with errors tending to be identified retrospectively; poor prescribing practices, drug wastage and a failure to promote NICE guidance and the National Service Framework. Some of the staff that planned, developed and implemented the project had come from Acute Hospitals and thus brought experience of more up-to-date systems. This knowledge, together with a commitment to providing a better service to patients and a desire for greater job satisfaction, helped with the initial planning.

Staffing changes

A new role of Dispensing Assistant (ATO) was created. The ATO took over dispensing duties and topped-up ward stock needs. Clinical pharmacy technicians

(CPT), who had previously undertaken these tasks, were trained as accredited checkers in the dispensary. The additional time available to them meant they could work at ward level, supporting clinical pharmacists and counselling and advising patients.

The new role of CPTs in turn released pharmacists for a clinical role. They were now able to underpin clinical governance, recommend prescribing decisions and simplify complex regimes.

Benefits

The key benefits identified include:

- Increased professional respect from consultants for all pharmacy staff
- Pharmacy staff feel able now to advise and challenge consultants on prescribing issues
- Culture of hospital more focused on improvements
- Success of project has had wider impact on hospital overall
- Greatly increased job satisfaction
- Pharmacy staff are able to use their skills and knowledge more effectively and hence take greater pleasure in their work. The staff are now more likely to remain in their employment, which therefore has a positive impact on previous retention and recruitment problems.
- Improved relationship between pharmacy staff and patients
- Having pharmacy staff on ward has given the service a 'human face'. Patients feel more confident in talking with pharmacists. Advice on medication from pharmacists may also be better received than that from doctors. Pharmacy staff feel patients may see them as 'independent' than doctors, lacking any 'ulterior motives' relating to a patient's treatment. This can be very important in the context of mental health.
- Reduced risk overall
- Closer monitoring and recording of side effects and adverse reactions
- Less scope for error – e.g., through individualised patient-dispensed medicines and detailed patient medication reviews on admission to hospital.
- Better use of other staff time
- Doctors and nurses now have reduced responsibility for medicines management issues, giving them more time to focus on other key responsibilities

Factors contributing to success

The enthusiasm and shared views of the core pharmacy team involved appear to have been the major factors in the success of the project.

The support of an 'excellent and innovative' Chief Executive was also crucial in engendering a culture for change within the hospital.

Good communication was key to all processes, including overcoming barriers. When problems emerged, large staff meetings were held, to ensure that everyone was kept in the picture and rumour was curtailed.

Issues and concerns

Staffing: Some long-serving staff had entrenched attitudes and it was initially difficult to persuade people to adapt. This issue largely resolved itself, through a combination of the persuasive powers of the Chief Pharmacist and project staff and older staff retiring. Training of staff for their new roles was very demanding and initially threatened to stifle progress with the new services. A major aspect of this was the requirement to develop Standard Operating Procedures, which hitherto were not available, within a limited time frame.

Fitting within pre-existing systems: The new arrangements within Pharmacy Services had knock-on effects for other work patterns and practices. There were some initial issues around the available space within the ward, which had been used by nursing staff and phlebotomists. Phlebotomists changed their working practices to accommodate the new presence of pharmacists on the ward.

Covering sickness and holidays: How the service would operate in the event of staff sickness and through annual leave was the one thing that had not been thought through fully. The new roles meant that there was little cross-cover to be called on and there were some difficulties in this area initially. However, these have since been resolved.

NHS Direct

Introduction

The NHS Direct telephone-based service offering information and advice on healthcare to the public, began as a pilot service launched by the Secretary of State for Health in 1998. The service now deals with over half a million calls per month in England and Wales. It has expanded into other media including the internet (NHS Direct Online, launched in 1999) and, recently, digital interactive TV (NHS Direct Interactive, launched in 2004), and provides a great deal of healthcare information on its web and digital TV sites. In March 2004 it was established as a special health authority, with its own board and staff.

The problem

The creation of NHS Direct was a response to an opportunity as much as a response to a problem. The general election of 1997 brought a Labour government to office.

After a long period in opposition, the new government planned to make significant changes to public services and began work on the preparation of a white paper[40] that would set out its plans for the NHS. In the Department of Health a number of working parties and 'brainstorming' events were given an explicit brief to develop new approaches and ideas. NHS Direct, which was conceived as making innovative use of already available modern information and communication technology (ICT) to improve public access to health information and advice, was born out of this process.

In the background was the report of previous work carried out under the then Chief Medical Officer[41]. As a review of emergency care outside hospital, it aimed to find ways of providing patients with access to appropriate care, while relieving pressure on existing services. It had been undertaken in response to the pressure of demand on accident and emergency services and on GPs. The work had resulted in a proposal to set up a telephone number, which would operate alongside 999 and be aimed at 'improving access and advice for the public in emergencies where people may not need the services of a 999 ambulance'. NHS Direct extended this concept to non-emergency services and to multiple communication channels (telephone, internet , digital TV).

The idea

The idea behind NHS Direct was to offer the public access, initially by telephone and in due course also through other modern communication channels, to professional healthcare information and advice, around the clock, every day of the year. The idea built on the successful development of telephone help-lines in many types of business e.g. insurance, but was a new application for the technology. NHS services had previously been available face-to-face only, with access to the majority of services via the patient's local, primary care services. The idea was that NHS Direct would give the public immediate access to nurses for advice and information by telephone, and change the public perception that getting access to NHS professionals was too often a slow and cumbersome process.

The innovation

The service provides professional healthcare information and advice to help the public manage their own health problems or, if necessary, to access the most appropriate care services. It sets out to improve the speed, quality and cost-effectiveness of NHS services by providing the most appropriate response to the user's needs and by reducing the unnecessary demands on other parts of the NHS.

How it happened

The preliminary idea, that more systematic and radical use of modern ICT should be considered as a key building block for a 'new NHS', was put forward in the discussions of a Department of Health working group on configuring health services, which had been formed to contribute to a forthcoming white paper on the NHS. This suggestion came from a member of the group who had previously been involved in 'brainstorming' discussions at regional level about new modes of service delivery, which had included the possibilities of using technology to improve public access. There was support for developing this line of thinking and the proposals for a new service began to take shape, with the working title of 'NHS Direct' being coined at an early stage.

An analysis of literature and other research showed that telephone help-lines were used successfully to provide medical advice in other countries comparable to the UK. The analysis provided useful information for shaping proposals for a service in England and reassurance that a service could work in a British context.

While still in an embryonic form, NHS Direct received the enthusiastic support of ministers. As a result, plans for the new service featured prominently in the white paper.

NHS Direct was developed quickly from the preliminary ideas to a fully operational service. Ideas were tested on the public, using research techniques and public consultation methods, and were well received. The three pilots which had been begun to be set up to test the proposal in the CMO's report were quickly adapted to become the first wave of NHS Direct pilots. The pilots, which were launched in March 1998, tested designs for the organisation and delivery of the service, based on features that were regarded as essential characteristics of the service: a universal telephone number, central management for what was to become a nationwide service, round-the-clock and year-round service, and all callers to be able to get access to a nurse, who was assisted by clinical decision support software. Further waves of NHS Direct site launches followed over the next two years. By November 2000 the service had met the 'new NHS' white paper target of being rolled out to cover the whole of England and Wales.

There was enthusiastic support from ministers who saw that the proposed service could fit well within their approach to modernising the NHS. Costings by the project team showed that the service could be provided for as little as £1–2 per head of the English population. Presenting the costings in this way strengthened the arguments for going ahead with development.

An initial review and analysis of related research confirmed the potential for the proposed service to be successful in the UK context. Public consultation produced evidence of public support for proposals, which was helpful in countering objections from some professional groups in the NHS. Later, monitoring of patient reactions to the service revealed very high levels of satisfaction, which was helpful in advocating the service to any groups who were sceptical about its value. Further support came from independent evaluation studies by Sheffield University and by the National Audit Office.

The piloting of the service was essential to test the innovation in operation. This enabled decisions to be made about the best delivery option and systems to be developed for managing and reducing risk (e.g. of users being given the wrong advice or of not following advice). The pilot also provided the time and opportunity to involve more people in the service and thus to build support for it, which put the service in a stronger position to deal with any problems that might develop at a later stage.

The proposed innovation appealed to different stakeholders for different reasons – as well as to the public and to ministers. For example, the nursing profession was supportive as the service offered new forms of employment and a high profile role to nurses.

There was a good mix of skills in the project team, which included a Department of Health Board level champion who could connect the proposals to other NHS policies and raise the proposal of the new service with senior audiences in the NHS and the Department of Health. The project team also included a strong operational research component, which helped the pilot to develop practical and efficient models for service delivery.

NHS Direct brought together different elements that were already tried and tested, although in different contexts. It was possible to research this experience and to learn from it. For example: the technology was in use in other contexts; it was possible to build on a clinical decision support system that was already in use in the US; and to learn from the experience of the public use of other helplines.

Challenges

Some members of some professional groups expressed concern about the quality of healthcare advice given over the telephone. Without seeing the patient, was it possible to be confident that the advice was appropriate or comprehensive? There was also concern about the possibility of generating new demand for primary care, from people who would use NHS Direct and then seek follow-up from their GP. In some cases, the objections of the primary care professionals were interpreted as objections to a new service that would challenge their previous monopoly on being a first port of call for healthcare advice in the NHS.

Ministerial and public support created a momentum to roll-out the service quickly. This brought the possibility that there would be insufficient time to pilot the new service thoroughly before having to make decisions about extending the coverage, thus increasing the risk of making mistakes that would expose the new service to criticism.

Gauging demand for such an innovative service was difficult. The project team decided to err on the side of caution and to use, to begin with, their higher estimates of potential demand, rather than to risk an early backlash when people tried to use the service but were unable to get through.

Police community support officers

The problem

From the late 1980s, awareness was beginning to emerge that it would be increasingly costly and impractical for the police to meet the rising public demand for a police presence on the streets, in the visible form of officers on patrol. This difficulty was also highlighted in the Audit Commission's paper, Streetwise – Effective Police Patrol in 1996. As the visible presence of police on the street either declined or was perceived by the public as declining, the work of the police would become increasingly hidden from public view.

This was in the context of a decrease in the number of other authority figures in public space – bus conductors and park wardens, for example. Neighbourhood or street wardens were being introduced in some areas to meet a similar need for security and reassurance, in response to a growing concern about anti-social behaviour. To meet the perceived gap in patrol services, a market was emerging for private patrol and security. A small number of local authorities were beginning to talk about developing their own security arrangements, separate from the police. If such a trend developed, especially in the public sector, it had the potential to alter fundamentally the role of the police in British society.

The idea

The idea of a different model of policing began to emerge. This was described as a 'horizontal model', which involved non-police officers carrying out patrol, while the police concentrated on other policing activities. The idea of 'police auxiliaries' as a patrolling force had been first developed in 2000 (in a run-up to a general election that year). At that time, there was little political will to take the idea forward. There was also resistance from the professional association of police officers, the Police Federation, who were opposed to what they saw as 'policing on the cheap'.

The innovation

A big step forward in the thinking came with ideas about limiting the powers of the proposed police auxiliaries and changing their name to police community support officers (PCSOs). For example, PCSOs were given limited powers to detain but not to arrest, and this helped to gain support for the proposals from the police profession.

How it happened

From the beginning, Sir Ian Blair (then Deputy Commissioner of the Metropolitan Police) was a key figure in the origination, development and promotion of the idea. He pursued a concept that was unpopular at first and faced much resistance. The commitment and support of such a senior figure enabled many internal objections and obstacles to the new development to be overcome.

The events of 11 September 2001 changed dramatically the environment for policing. The terrorist attacks in the USA meant that the need for increased public security shot up the political and public agenda in London and elsewhere. There was a sudden increase in demand for police officers to carry out patrol duties in central London. Levels of street crime rose elsewhere as police officers were re-located to the areas that were regarded as prime targets for terrorists. Many police officers began to see the potential advantages of officers being released from central London security patrols, so that they could focus their efforts on other matters.

Political support for developing the concept of PCSOs increased quickly after 9/11, and a significant sum of money was made available by central government to develop and implement plans for the new workforce. Provision for the employment of PCSOs was made in the Police Reform Act of 2002. A small project team was set up to develop the plans, with a steering group that included two members of the Metropolitan Police Authority.

The scale of the funding allowed the plans to be implemented on a larger scale than had originally been envisaged as a first stage. The first PCSOs were working in London by September 2002. By December 2003, there were 3,243 in England and Wales (figures from Home Office website).

Challenges

There were two significant barriers that needed to be overcome in order for the concept to be realised.

There was significant resistance in the early days from the Police Federation, the professional membership body for police officers, who initially saw the proposals as a threat to members' interests and to the professional values and strength of the police service. They feared that PCSOs would be given similar powers to police officers, but be cheaper to recruit and employ.

There was also difficulty with the nature of the organisational structures, policies and procedures within the police force, as different functions (e.g. HR, uniform design) sought to apply their established approaches to the new group of staff and type of work. These approaches tended to be slow and threatened to impede progress towards the introduction of PCSOs.

What helped

A number of factors were significant in overcoming these barriers and facilitating the rapid development of the new workforce.

The continuing leadership by Sir Ian Blair was critical in promoting the proposals and in overcoming obstacles in the development and implementation process. Some members of the Metropolitan Police Authority were influential advocates for the proposals.

There was a small but strong implementation team, comprising individuals with complementary skills, which had the capacity and commitment to develop the concept. The team had been formed from within the Metropolitan Police, thereby providing it with knowledge of the police and credibility with police colleagues.

Throughout the development and implementation process, the core team maintained the established principle that PCSOs would have a distinct role from that of the police. Any dilution – real or perceived – of that principle would have reinforced the anxieties of the Police Federation and others.

The funding from the Home Office enabled the project team to work somewhat outside the usual procedures of the Metropolitan Police and therefore to move more quickly. For example, after an initial and unsuccessful attempt by the in-house designers at designing new PCSO uniforms, the team brought in external designers. This was a radical departure for the organisation and acted as a catalyst for change, with the final uniforms being designed successfully in-house.

Similarly, the team took the lead in drafting terms and conditions and employment contracts for the PCSOs. These were significantly different from usual police arrangements. For example, flexible working arrangements were introduced to attract a greater diversity of applicants and no minimum level of qualifications was required for acceptance as a recruit.

Significant attention was paid to publicity and promotion of the emerging concept. The team carried out a great deal of consultation and much lobbying within the police force in order to facilitate acceptance. They prepared the ground for the arrival of PCSOs by giving local police the responsibility for the introduction and management of PCSOs in their area, for which they were given training.

There was a heavy emphasis on external communication as well. Communication through the media, throughout all stages of the project, raised public awareness.

Impact: unforeseen consequences

The approach taken by the implementation team became a catalyst for the development of new ways of working in the Metropolitan Police. For example, the introduction of different types of terms and conditions showed that new ways of doing business could be successful.

The diversity of PCSOs, in ethnicity, education levels, age and background has far surpassed initial expectations.

Project 218

Introduction

This case study from the Scottish criminal justice system provides an example of a new type of service being provided for a newly emerging client group, as the result of a crisis. Clear shortcomings in the existing system, and the lack of viable alternatives, created a space in which a new approach could be tested. The initiative is resource intensive, but is far more cost-effective than the alternative of short-term custodial sentences and a cycle of re-offending. Like the Manchester City Centre Safe example, the focus is on identifying and treating the causes of the problem, rather than merely dealing with the symptoms.

The problem

A crisis in part of the Scottish prison prompted the recognition of women offenders as a separate client group, requiring tailored services to meet their particular needs. A spate of suicides at Cornton Vale prison in Glasgow between 1995 and 1997 prompted a major review of community disposals and the use of custody for women offenders in Scotland. An Inter-Agency Forum on Women's Offending (1998 – 2000) was established to better understand the problems contributing to women offending and to seek new solutions for Glasgow. The Forum recommended practical measures to tackle the causes of women's crime. In December 2000 the Ministerial Group on Women's Offending was established to take forward this work and implement a package of measures designed to reduce the number of women held in custody in Scotland. High volumes of women were being received into prison for short periods of time. Research showed that short prison sentences were not successful in terms of helping women to move on and to prevent further offending, and made it difficult for women to resettle back into communities.

The idea

The Ministerial Group's efforts were underpinned by the recognition that the pattern of women's offending frequently begins in social, economic and emotional problems occurring early in life, and that a concerted effort across agencies in the statutory and voluntary sectors was needed to address these issues. The Group argued that, given the pattern of offending, the majority of women could be dealt with more effectively in a community setting, using the increasing range of disposals available to the courts. They also sought to provide women offenders with ready access to services and facilities to help them address their problems within the community, creation of services to meet the specific needs of women, and a focus on relationship building as part of this process.

The Inter-Agency Forum had suggested that a 'Time Out' Centre be considered in Glasgow to provide a range of residentially or non-residentially based support services for women. The Ministerial Group took forward the proposal for a Time Out centre, which would offer the courts a specialist, community-based facility for women.

The innovation

Time Out at 218 was officially opened in January 2004. The service offers programmes of care, support and development designed to stop women offending by tackling the substance misuse, trauma and poverty that drive it. The project is funded by the Scottish Executive and Glasgow City Council Criminal Justice service and supported by Glasgow City Council Social Work department.

Glasgow City Council hosts the service and managed the service contracting, which involved a process of public tender. Turning Point Scotland, which had been running Turnaround, a programme for women drug users in the criminal justice system, won the bid and manages the service. Time Out at 218 incorporates and expands the services previously offered by Turnaround.

How it happened

Turnaround had been set up as a seedbed project, managed by Turning Point Scotland, to explore what worked in terms of service provision for female offenders. It piloted Scotland's first diversion programme for women drug users in Glasgow, providing an alternative to prosecution involving regular participation in one-to-one and group sessions. This was one of several experimental approaches set up in reaction to the crisis in Cornton Vale, and achieved positive results, while operating on a relatively small scale between 1995 and 2003. Through practical experience the project established what worked for individual service users and built up a store of good practice. These methods and approaches were reinforced by the research findings emerging from the Ministerial Group.

On winning the tender, the Turning Point Scotland team found itself with a clear set of goals and targets, that needed to be translated into practical implementation plans, informed by models of practice and appropriately resourced. The management team met over a series of development days and brainstormed how to put the ideas and recommendations into practice, drawing on the academic and policy research, the team's collective experience, and consultation with colleagues in other agencies. The starting point for service development was to visualise in detail the experience the team wanted women to have at the project. Through this process, the team developed three service programmes, a design for the use and style of the building, a staff profile, training profile and core project values for all staff.

Challenges

Efforts to increase the use of custodial arrangements in favour of prison sentences required a comprehensive culture change in existing systems. Courts had to be convinced of the value of imposing the most effective penalties toward changing future behaviour rather simply handing down punishment. Despite an increase in alternatives to custody, the courts were still choosing to remand high numbers of women and impose short custodial sentences for minor offences and fine default.

For Time Out to work, it needed to be part of a network of community support, with criminal justice social workers supporting community disposals, and joint working across the relevant public and voluntary sector agencies to provide women with the support needed to function effectively within their communities. A specialist service would also be needed in Glasgow to link with women offenders during and after their time with Time Out and act as a care manager in designated cases.

What helped

Time Out had the backing of all major stakeholders at ministerial level, as represented in the multi-agency Ministerial Group that endorsed the project. In setting up the group, the Scottish Executive had also demonstrated its commitment to changing Scotland's approach to women offenders.

The approach is based on a solid combination of research and theory, and practical knowledge gained over time through the experience of Turnaround, all of which point to the importance of relationships as a core element in working with women offenders.

Impact and issues

Time Out, as an alternative to custody, provides the support and opportunity for women to move on from crises and re-integrate into society. Admission to the day service is mainly through referral by criminal justice services including the Court, police and social work services. Women may also self refer for an assessment. The centre offers safety, support accessing services, and a focus on the treatment of problems. There is day programme of on-going assessment, counselling, support, advocacy and group work. Fourteen residential places are also available as appropriate, for periods up to twelve weeks. A comprehensive psychological and physical health team, run by the Greater Glasgow NHS Board, is attached to the service.

The team believes that 'the vision is coming to life.' The building in which the service is housed departs from any preconceived notions of down-at-the-heel rehabilitation centres, and offers a bright, well designed and beautifully decorated space in which women can feel safe and comfortable. Services are provided according to what staff, informed by research, good practice and service users believe drug services for women should look like, rather than what convention might dictate. Programmes are designed around women's core needs.

The three programmes are working well and having a big impact on individual women's lives. More women are achieving success and sustainability than was expected at this early stage in the project. Availability of residential and day support in the same building, with the programmes available in both areas, has allowed women to be supported more fully and more smoothly without loss of continuity.

The inclusion of the health team provides expertise in psychology, mental health and physical health, and effective links to community based resources. Programmes of activity and engagement are taking place through encouragement rather than coercion. The centre makes full use of alternative therapies such as acupuncture, head massage and other relaxation techniques, which has facilitated a low use of sleep medication and chemical relaxants.

However, it remains a challenge to convince all the components of the criminal justice system that the problem of women offenders requires time to resolve. Many women will continue to fall foul of the system before the efforts of Time Out bear fruit. The service is gradually winning the support of the Courts, but many of the women with whom it works require sustained work, together with a genuine belief in their ability to turn their circumstances around.

St George's Mental Health Trust

Introduction

The idea in this example drew upon innovative practice observed elsewhere, but adapted it to suit a particular context. The underlying objective was to create employment opportunities for people often excluded from the labour market. It was possible to develop the initiative without a large investment of resources. It did however involve significant risk, and considerable potential for resistance from staff and the wider public. It was particularly creative in identifying a problem facing the NHS, identifying a problem facing a particular client group, and reconfiguring these two problems to create a solution.

The problem

People with experience of mental health problems are far less likely to be in employment. Research has shown that employment plays an important role in enhancing and maintaining good mental health and quality of life in people who have experienced such problems. The NHS is the largest employer in Europe, and suffers from a shortage of staff. Reluctance to employ users of mental health users excludes a significant section of society from filling vacancies.

The idea

In 1993, Dr Rachel Perkins, a senior employee at St George's Mental Health Trust was granted a fellowship to observe innovative mental health programmes in the US. The programmes she visited included one in Colorado that employed service users as staff in mental health services. The programme supported 40 people working in specially created posts. On her return to the UK, she sought to introduce a similar approach. Rather than creating special posts, however, she sought to use current vacancies within the hospital.

The innovation

Following a pilot in 1995, a large-scale user employment scheme was introduced in 1997 to open all job opportunities across the trust to mental health users. The scheme offers people who have mental health problems support to gain and sustain employment in existing posts within the trust. Mental health users are encouraged to apply for positions within the trust in a number of ways:

- Every person specification states that personal experience of mental health problems is desirable, in addition to other qualifications, experience and personal attributes as required for the post.
- An equal opportunities statement is included on all job advertisements, encouraging applications from people who have experienced mental health problems.
- All job packs include information about the programme, so that support can be sought throughout the application process.

The trust has also established a work experience programme aimed at people with mental illnesses who do not have any prior experience of work, or are unsure of whether they want to work in the mental health field. The programme is funded by Jobcentre Plus and involves 10 weeks of work preparation, and assistance in finding a job, within or external to the trust.

How it happened

After her return from the USA in late 1993, Dr Perkins put the idea to top level management and was able to convince the Chief Executives of the hospital and health authority, together with the Assistant Director for Social Services at the local authority, of its merits. Funding was acquired. In the pilot stage, six mental health users were recruited to part time posts that did not require specific qualifications. The position holders were given a support worker whilst they were at work, and a detailed task analysis of each job was created.

The success of the pilot saw the programme rolled out across the whole trust, including positions requiring qualifications, in 1997. The pilot had shown that individuals preferred not to have constant support and supervision. The scheme was therefore amended to provide support as needed, for example through telephone contact. The programme again proved successful and was further extended in 2004 to include access to professional qualification courses, run in conjunction with a local university.

Challenges

The major challenge was to change staff members' perceptions of the programme. Some required a great deal of persuasion. Prior to the extension of the scheme, every staff group was given the opportunity to air their views and fears. The pilot programme's success played a huge part in altering people's views, as they could see for themselves that the approach could work.

What helped

Within the organisation, the support of top-level management for the idea was crucial to carrying it forward. Senior support meant that the idea could be effectively sold to the organisation as a whole, and the management proved receptive to change. The initial pilot was rolled out on a very small scale, so that any problems could be ironed out before it was extended.

Externally, the positive coverage that the scheme received in the national media also contributed to its success. The programme also tied in with a new government priority to increase the employment opportunities for those with mental health problems, helping to secure support.

Impact and issues

The programme has had a positive impact for both users and the organisation. To date, the trust has supported over 100 people in existing posts on standard terms and conditions, and provided short-term work preparation for 32 people. In 2004 the programme supported two employees in secondments in professional clinical training at a local university. The programme provides participants with opportunities that would previously have been out of their reach: 'The difference it makes to people's lives is absolutely immense. Their confidence is shot to pieces, they really feel they are never going to work again.'

The programme has also changed the culture within the trust, breaking down the 'them and us' barriers between patients and staff and creating an environment where mental health issues can be openly expressed. St George's advises other trusts around the country about setting up their own programmes, facilitated with funding from the Department of Health. The trust also runs open days for those wishing to find out more, which attract about 80 people at a time. The programme has attracted considerable international interest, and Denmark has implemented a similar scheme.

The Urban Village

The context

'*How we live our lives is shaped by where we live our lives.*' – John Prescott, Deputy Prime Minister[42]

Throughout the 1990s, there was growing awareness that adequate housing means more than just bricks and mortar. 'Where we live our lives' extends beyond the building where we eat and sleep to include the availability of health, education and transport services, the social mix in our neighbourhood, how safe we feel, inside our homes and on the streets and how clean and well-lit the streets are.

In 1999, the number of officially homeless people across London was approximately 25,000. Organisations working with and for homeless people estimate that there are more than 400,000 'hidden homeless' people in England, sleeping in rough or temporary accommodation, with friends or acquaintances.[43] The Prime Minister set a target to reduce the numbers of people sleeping rough to as near zero as possible but by at least two thirds by 2002. The Rough Sleepers Unit was established within the DETR in April 1999, headed by the 'homelessness czar'. Reports were written on the lack of access to health care amongst homeless people.

Hostel accommodation, the usual solution for single homeless people, was coming under scrutiny too. Crisis was uncomfortable about expecting people to live in places where conditions were as poor as they were in many hostels. Many of them were not places where people could begin to shape a life for themselves and Crisis began to look for a better solution, which went beyond a bed for the night and addressed the wider needs of homeless people. They wanted to provide support as well as accommodation, so that homeless people could shape a better life.

'We must find ways of providing homeless people with supportive environments in which they can begin to confront their problems and regain control of their lives.'

Shaks Ghosh, Chief Executive, Crisis[44]

At the same time, concern was rising over the exodus of key workers from London. A dearth of affordable housing left nurses, firemen and other public sector and low income workers with the choice of commuting long distances or moving out of London altogether. The Mayor of London set up a commission to report on the requirement for affordable housing in London. The report, Homes for a World City, commented on the links between the availability of affordable housing and reducing homelessness. In his Foreword to the Report, published in May 2000, the Chair of the Commission, Chris Holmes, highlighted 'the importance of the connections between providing affordable homes and other key priorities – especially in health, education, transport and employment.' [45]

Crisis and the King's Fund, the two organisations involved from the beginning in what would eventually become the Urban Village project, were at the heart of these discussions. Shaks Ghosh, Chief Executive at Crisis, was 'in the market for a good idea' that would address her concerns over hostel accommodation and the 'revolving door' syndrome that sees people going from street to hostel and back to the street. The King's Fund was about to launch its Health and Regeneration Programme, one of the aims of which was to increase the active involvement of health workers in urban regeneration. Independently of each other, Crisis and the King's Fund learned of Common Ground, a project in New York's Time's Square.

The idea

'Common Ground is a non-profit housing and community development organisation whose mission is to solve homelessness … [that] provides a comprehensive support system designed to help people regain lives of stability and independence.'[46] Driven by its founder and President, Rosanne Haggerty, Common Ground has grown since 1991, when it began work on its original site at the Times Square Hotel in New York. Its replication programme provides assistance to other organisations wishing to develop supportive housing. It has developed other types of accommodation, all including support services, to address the different needs of homeless people and has started to look now at prevention as well as cure.

The innovation

The key innovations in the Common Ground project are the provision of support services on-site and mixed tenancies. Homeless and low-income people live in the same building, in single-occupancy units. There is an emphasis on training and providing real jobs for people and the support they need to hold on to them. Support is available for people to address issues that may impact on the particular community as a whole – e.g., drug or alcohol dependency.

The inspiration

All partners in the London project mentioned how important Rosanne Haggerty had been to Common Ground in New York. She was recognised as the inspirational driving force behind the project and her vision helped to seed enthusiasm for the idea in London.

Common Ground comes to London

Crisis and the King's Fund decided to work together to bring Common Ground to London. Following a competitive tender, London and Quadrant Housing Trust became the third partner. In November 2000, the partnership was announced, the project described as Common Ground (London) and the intention was to build 200 studio flats.

The announcement was made a week after the Urban White Paper and the project fitted in well with the priorities identified there, which included the revival of city centres and the development of more mixed communities.

The London context gave the project slightly different priorities. For example, whilst health was important to the NY project, especially for drug users, it was never an explicit objective. In the UK, the King's Fund developed a programme for health promotion as part of the project, which fit in with their wider aims of reducing health inequalities and improving public health.

Citywell

Following some initial problems in defining the nature of their partnership, the three organisations formed an independent organisation, Citywell, to see the project forward. The Citywell board comprised two members from each of the three partners and an independent chair. The Board was formed with the hope of clarifying leadership on the project and was seen at first as a new start. However, problems with the partnership continued and the project lost focus. In the absence of a strong direction and leadership, other difficulties proved impossible to resolve. A suitable site was hard to find and once a possible site was located, community suspicion and political antipathy, combined with changes in the funding regime, finally proved too much and the partnership was dissolved.

Barriers

The barriers to the success of the Citywell project fell into four broad categories:

- Idea transfer
- Planning
- Partnership
- Support

Idea transfer: In transferring the idea of supportive mixed housing from New York to London, the partnership needed to consider whether differences between the two environments would impact upon the project, and how.

The rental and housing markets in the US are very different to that in the UK. Two particular areas were relevant to the project. First, the tax credit system in New York provides State tax credits for owners of housing for persons of low-income. This would have been of financial benefit to the London project. Crisis approached Paul Boetang, then at the Treasury, to talk about the possibility of introducing tax credits in this country. Whilst they were rebuffed on this issue, they did discover that the Treasury had, independently, sent a team to look at Common Project and were offered other support.

The homelessness problem in New York is much more widespread than in London and the social and public support for homeless people is limited. The need for an initiative to provide positive support was stark. In London, it was less so. The first purpose-built foyer project had opened in 1993, to be followed by many more; for some people, the idea behind Common Ground was not sufficiently distant from foyers to excite their interest or support.

It was also important to consider cultural differences. For some within Crisis these were seen as sufficiently large to make it inappropriate to transfer the idea. However, this may have been just one more element in a 'general organisational resistance to new ideas' identified by Shaks Ghosh of Crisis: 'People will keep telling you it can't happen.'

Finally, but perhaps most importantly, the idea needed to transfer not just on paper and in practice but psychologically too. Talking about the evolution of the idea, Shaks Ghosh noted that initially, the project was thought of as 'they're doing this great thing in NY and we'd like to do one in London'. It needed to become 'we're going to do this great thing in London and by the way there's one in NY'. The move was from admiring somebody else's project, to making a commitment to your own.

Planning: Lack of initial planning lay behind many of the difficulties encountered by the Citywell Partnership. The partnership itself was not well planned, which meant that resolving problems and assigning responsibilities was difficult. Lack of planning meant too that problems were not anticipated and so not headed off before they arose.

A financial plan was drawn up for the Citywell project but a business case, argued in policy terms, was not developed. The case for bringing Common Ground to London, whilst perhaps clear to the partner organisations, was not made more widely. How the idea differed from existing projects in the UK and the precise nature of its fit with other current agenda, such as health promotion and addressing homelessness, was thus not readily apparent to potential supporters. Information management was not adequate and news of the project leaked out before it was officially launched, catching Citywell on the back foot.

Insufficient planning made coping with the unforeseen difficult. For example, the NHS, who owned the site in which Citywell was interested, were slow to make up their minds whether or not to sell and on what basis they might sell. In addition to this, the planning regulations changed mid-way through negotiations on the site, presenting a further setback.

Partnership: The three organisations had very different working cultures. The roles of each within the partnership, the nature of the partnership itself and of the leadership required were not as tightly defined as they might have been. The idea began to lose shape and focus and the lack of leadership meant that no one was able to bring it back on track.

Support: One thing that had not been anticipated was the lack of support for the project from the community around the site initially identified as suitable. The community felt that it was being lumbered with 'just another hostel.' Regeneration of the King's Cross area had already displaced drug and prostitution problems into the area and Citywell was seen as adding to these. Some local councillors were antagonistic too.

Lack of external support and the resistance against it added to the existing difficulties, taking up time and resources as well as having sapping the energy needed to see through a new project.

The absence of a single dedicated and passionate project leader was perhaps a crucial factor in the difficulties in building support. The partnership had no full time 'Rosanne Haggerty' figure. Her enthusiasm seems to have been instrumental in selling the idea to the original partners.

The Urban Village

Despite the difficulties encountered by the Citywell team, King's Fund and Crisis remained committed to the idea. Following a donation of £3.6 million from Dave Gilmour, (a musician), funding from the Housing Corporation and a new Chairman who wanted to know what 'the big idea was', Crisis decided to revive the project. The King's Fund stayed involved and they were joined by a new housing partner, Genesis. With the forming of the new partnership, the project name was changed to The Urban Village.

Learning from experience

A lot had been learned from the Citywell experience. First, a more strategic approach to partnership was adopted and the different organisational cultures and expertises were used to advantage, rather than clashing. These different roles allowed the project to reach a wide range of audiences, building credibility for the project.

There was increased awareness of the risks too. A full business case was developed and presented to the outside world, helping them to bring in other partners and build a support base. By this time, each of the partners knew where their strengths lay and how they could best contribute to the partnership as a whole.

One of the key partners was the Housing Corporation (HC), who had been involved in the project from the start, including the initial study visit to New York. They had provided the King's Fund and Crisis with advice in selecting a housing association partner and were keen to support innovations. The HC was also in the process of changing its own internal culture, seeking to become more strategic and fleet of foot, looking to explore new ideas and to take more flexible and pragmatic approaches to innovation. It saw its relation to the project as that of an investor, committing itself to up to £20m support for the project, and rolling this commitment forward as the project developed, giving the project the security of knowing that a significant proportion of the capital funding was already in place.

As an investor, the HC wanted to be sure that the big questions had been considered; that the project was thought of in terms of outcomes, not just of housing units; that no compromise was made on design and that sustainability, as well as set up, was being considered. Urban Village needed to show the HC that they had thought through the problems, developed solutions and had an exit strategy in case things went wrong for a second time. Within this framework, the HC gave the project team the freedom to develop their ideas about what they would do and how. This, together with the learning from Citywell and an experienced project manager, provided the discipline and flexibility needed for the project to regain impetus.

Impact and issues

The factors identified by the partners as important to the Urban Village project's success (and at this point, it looks as though it will be successful) include:

- Careful consideration of how the idea will transfer – stripping it back to fundamentals and shaping it more closely to the London context
- Spending more time getting buy-in within the partner organisations
- Choosing partners with the right expertise
- Making sure all roles and responsibilities are clearly understood
- Good project management
- Champions 'to see you through the dull phases' and promote the project to 'the great and the good'.
- Knowing your limitations

Appendix B: Assessing your organisation's potential for creativity

Ask these questions about your organisation, or your part of it, and the answers will give you some important indicators of its capacity to be creative:

- Is there enough 'slack' in the system to allow people time and space to think and to be in contact with people with different perspectives and experiences? Or do people work under too much pressure too much of the time? Are there processes or arrangements that could be changed or scaled down to free up time for more creative purposes?
- Are managers receptive to ideas from staff, including ideas that appear unconventional or infeasible? Are managers ready to question assumptions and to accept this from staff?
- Do the accountability, appraisal and performance management systems recognise the value of ideas (including unsuccessful ones), of leadership for creativity and of risk management? Does the organisation value 'useful failure'?
- Is there an approach to recruitment that brings together people with diverse professional backgrounds and an approach to capacity building that gives staff experience of work or tasks outside the responsibilities of their jobs?
- Are senior managers able to protect the organisation and its staff from too many of the disruptive effects of policy and organisational change and to provide a consistent and long-term vision?
- Are people in the organisation sufficiently skilled at 'managing up' – at aligning their ideas and objectives with political agendas and other organisations' priorities?
- Is the organisation prepared to allow sufficient time for innovations to show results? Is there a culture of learning from pilots and evaluation, including open discussion of unexpected outcomes?
- Are risk management and risk assessment skills and systems strong enough to support creativity and innovation?

Appendix C: Members of the Public Interest Research Group 2003

Dr Sheila Adam,
  North East London Strategic Health Authority
David Albury
Professor John Benington
  Warwick Institute of Governance and Public Management
Sir Michael Bichard
  The London Institute
Commander Cressida Dick
  Metropolitan Police Service
Ian Hughes
  London Borough of Southwark
Ms Pat Kneen
  Joseph Rowntree Foundation
Professor Gloria Laycock
  The Jill Dando Institute of Crime Science
Clare Matterson
  The Wellcome Trust
Anne Page
Dr Barry Quirk
  London Borough of Lewisham
Stephen Thornton
  Health Foundation

Bibliography

Teresa M Amabile, Constance N Hadley, Steven J Kramer, 'Creativity under the Gun', in *The Innovative Enterprise*, Harvard Business Review, August 2002

S Borins, *The challenge of innovating in government*, PriceWaterhouseCoopers Endowment for the Business of Government, Arlington, Va, USA (2002)

Nigel Crouch, 'DTI: Extract on Report on Partnerships with People (PwP) and Living Innovation programmes' in *Managing Best Practice* 88 The Industrial Society, October 2001

Richard Farson and Ralph Keyes, 'The Failure-Tolerant Leader', in *Harvard Business Review*, August 2002

Jean Hartley, 'Innovation in governance and public services, past and present' in *Public Money and Management,* January 2005

Industrial Society, 'Managing Innovation' in *Managing Best Practice* No. 88 October 2001 (also reported on The Work Foundation website February 2002) http://www.theworkfoundation.com/newsroom/archivereleases.jsp?ref=20

Arthur Koestler, *The Act of Creation*, Hutchinson, 1964

Charles Landry, *Creative Lewisham*, Lewisham Culture and Urban Development Commission, 2003

Charles Leadbeater, *The Man in the Caravan and other stories*, IDEA 2003

Tom Ling, *Innovation: Lessons from the private sector*, A think piece in support of the Invest to Safe Study, November 2002, National Audit Office

Living Innovation website, http://www.livinginnovation.org/alternative.html

Alex McKie, Extract from Futures Report: 'Creativity in business – buzzword or bottom line?' in *Managing Best Practice* 88 The Industrial Society, October 2001

Mark H Moore, *Accounting for change: Reconciling the demands for accountability and innovation in the public sector*, Council for Excellence in Government Washington DC 1993

Geoff Mulgan and David Albury, *Innovation in the Public Sector*, Prime Minister's Strategy Unit, October 2003 http://www.strategy.gov.uk/downloads/files/pubinov2.pdf

National Audit Office, *Supporting innovation: managing risk in government departments* HC 864 1999-2000, Stationery Office

The NHS Modernisation Agency, *The Healthcare Innovation Toolkit: how to generate and implement creative ideas for service improvement*, The NHS Modernisation Agency, 2004

Paul Plsek and Lynne Maher, Discussion Paper on Innovation, for the NHS Modernisation Agency SMT meeting, May 2004

A Rajan and B Martin, Extract from 'Harnessing Creativity to Improve the Bottom Line', The Chartered Institute of Management Accountants (CIMA), in *Managing Best Practice* No. 88 The Industrial Society, October 2001

Horst W J Rittel and Melvin M Webber, 'Dilemmas in a general theory of planning', in *Policy Sciences* 4 (1973) pp155–169

Ken Robinson, *Learning to be creative*, Capstone 2001 Oxford

Peter Senge, *The Fifth Discipline: the art and practice of the learning organization*, Random House Business Books 1993

Rajesh Sethi, Daniel C Smith and C Whan Park, 'How to Kill a Team's Creativity', in *The Innovative Enterprise*, Harvard Business Review, August 2002

Jane Steele Wasted Values: *Harnessing the commitment of public managers*, Public Management Foundation 1999

M Walker and E Jeanes, (1999) *Innovation in a Regulated Service: The Case of English Housing Associations*, Cardiff University/University of Exeter

M Walker, E Jeanes and R Rowlands, *Measuring innovation – applying the literature-based innovation output indicator to public services*, Cardiff University/University of Exeter

M West, 'Creativity and Innovation at Work' in *The Psychologist*, Vol 13, no 9, September 2000, pp460–464

Endnotes

1 Charles Landry, *Creative Lewisham*, Lewisham Culture and Urban Development Commission, 2003

2 Ken Robinson, *Learning to be Creative,* Capstone 2001 Oxford

3 M West, 'Creativity and Innovation at Work' in *The Psychologist*, Vol 13, no 9, September 2000, p460 – 464

4 Northern Ireland Department of Culture, Arts and Leisure, Creativity Unit, *All Our Futures,* 1999

5 The National Advisory Committee on Creative and Cultural Education, *All our futures: Creativity, culture and education*, DfEE, 1999, p29 http://www.ncaction. org.uk/creativity/resources.htm

6 Paul Plsek and Lynne Maher, Discussion Paper on Innovation, for the NHS Modernisation Agency SMT meeting, May 2004

7 Arthur Koestler *The Act of Creation*, Hutchinson, 1964

8 The National Advisory Committee on Creative and Cultural Education, *All our futures: Creativity, culture and education*, op.cit

9 Jean Hartley, 'Innovation in governance and public services, past and present' in *Public Money and Management,* January 2005

10 Teresa M Amabile, Constance N Hadley, Steven J Kramer, 'Creativity under the Gun', in 'The Innovative Enterprise', *Harvard Business Review*, August 2002

11 Nigel Crouch, DTI: Extract from 'Report on Partnerships with People (PwP) and Living Innovation programmes' in *Managing Best Practice* 88 The Industrial Society, October 2001

12 Richard Farson and Ralph Keyes, 'The Failure-Tolerant Leader', in the *Harvard Business Review*, August 2002

13 Tom Ling, *Innovation: Lessons from the private sector*, a think piece in support of the Invest to Save Study, November 2002, National Audit Office

14 Industrial Society, *Managing Innovation Managing Best Practice* No. 88 October 2001 (also reported on The Work Foundation website February 2002) http://www.theworkfoundation.com/newsroom/archivereleases.jsp?ref=20

15 Geoff Mulgan and David Albury *Innovation in the Public Sector,* Prime Minister's Strategy Unit, October 2003 http://www.strategy.gov.uk/downloads/files/pubinov2.pdf

16 Tom Ling, op.cit

17 Horst W J Rittel and Melvin M Webber, 'Dilemmas in a general theory of planning' in *Policy Sciences* 4 (1973) 155-169

18. M Walker and E Jeanes, *Innovation in a Regulated Service: The Case of English Housing Associations*, Cardiff University/University of Exeter, 1999

19 Jane Steele, *Wasted Values: Harnessing the commitment of public managers* Public Management Foundation, 1999

20 S Borins, *The challenge of innovating in government,* PriceWaterhouseCoopers Endowment for the Business of Government, Arlington, Va, USA (2002)

21 Industrial Society, Managing Innovation *Managing Best Practice* No. 88 October 2001 (also reported on The Work Foundation website February 2002) http://www.theworkfoundation.com/newsroom/archivereleases.jsp?ref=20

22 Living Innovation website http://www.livinginnovation.org

23 The NHS Modernisation Agency, *The Healthcare Innovation Toolkit: how to generate and implement creative ideas for service improvement*, The NHS Modernisation Agency, 2004

24 Professor A Rajan and B Martin, Extract from 'Harnessing Creativity to Improve the Bottom Line', The Chartered Institute of Management Accountants (CIMA), in *Managing Best Practice* No. 88 The Industrial Society, October 2001

25 Living Innovation website, http://www.livinginnovation.org/alternative.html

26 Tom Ling, November 2002, citing Peter Senge

27 Rajesh Sethi, Daniel C Smith and C Whan Park, 'How to Kill a Team's Creativity', in *The Innovative Enterprise*, Harvard Business Review, August 2002

28 Geoff Mulgan and David Albury, *Innovation in the Public Sector*, Prime Minister's Strategy Unit, October 2003 http://www.strategy.gov.uk/downloads/files/pubinov2.pdf

29 A Rajan and B Martin, extract from Harnessing Creativity to Improve the Bottom Line, The Chartered Institute of Management Accountants (CIMA), in *Managing Best Practice* no. 88 The Industrial Society, October 2001

30 Tom Ling, November 2002

31 National Audit Office, *Supporting Innovation: Managing risk in government departments*, HC 864 NAO, 2000, p.4-6.

32 Geoff Mulgan and David Albury, *Innovation in the Public Sector*, Prime Minister's Strategy Unit, October 2003 http://www.strategy.gov.uk/downloads/files/pubinov2.pdf

33 Mark H Moore, *Accounting for change: Reconciling the demands for accountability and innovation in the public sector*, Council for Excellence in Government Washington DC 1993

34 National Audit Office, *Supporting innovation: managing risk in government departments* HC 864 1999-2000, Stationery Office

35 Extract from Alex McKie's Futures Report: 'Creativity in business – buzzword or bottom line?' in *Managing Best Practice* 88 The Industrial Society, October 2001

36 Nigel Crouch, DTI: Extract on Report on Partnerships with People (PwP) and Living Innovation programmes in *Managing Best Practice* 88 The Industrial Society, October 2001

37 Charles Leadbeater, *The Man in the Caravan* and other stories, IDEA 2003

38 Groundwork is a federation of trusts in England, Wales and Northern Ireland, working with their partners to improve the quality of the local environment, the lives of local people and the success of local businesses in areas in need of investment and support.

39 MTAs are 'a cross between nursing and pathology staff'

40 Department of Health, *The New NHS*, 1997

41 Developing emergency services in the community, 1997

42 Foreword to the Urban White Paper, *Our Towns and Cities: the future*, November 2000 http://www.odpm.gov.uk/stellent/groups/odpm_urbanpolicy/documents/page/odpm_urbpol_608358.hcsp

43 http://www.homelesspages.org.uk

44 Foreword, *A Future Foretold, New Approaches to Meeting the Long Term Needs of Single Homeless People*, Gerard Lemos, Research by Gill Goodby, Crisis, 1999

45 http://www.london.gov.uk/mayor/housing_commission/

46 http://www.commonground.org/